john ackerman

listening to god

SPIRITUAL FORMATION IN CONGREGATIONS

FOREWORD BY ALICE MANN

the alban institute

Scripture quotations, unless otherwise noted, are from the New Revised Standard Version of the Bible, copyright © 1989, Division of Christian Education of the National Council of Churches of Christ in the United States of America, and are used by permission.

Scripture quotations marked TM are from *The Message*, a paraphrase of the Bible by Eugene H. Peterson, copyright © 1993, 1994, 1995, and are used by permission of NavPress Publishing Group.

Scripture quotations marked KIV are from the Holy Bible, King James Version.

The chart on page 3, "Hierarchy versus the Circle," is adapted from *Spirit at Work*, by Jay Conger, copyright © 1994, and is used by permission of Jossey-Bass, Inc., a subsidiary of John Wiley & Sons, Inc.

The figures titled "The Objectivist Myth of Knowing" and "The Community of Truth" in chapter 1 come from *The Courage to Teach: Exploring the Inner Landscape of a Teacher's Life*, by Parker Palmer, copyright © 1998, and are reprinted by permission of Jossey-Bass, Inc., a subsidiary of John Wiley & Sons, Inc.

The "Spiritual Style Sorter" on page 48 is the work of Corinne Ware, and is used with her permission.

NOTE TO READER: *Charts in this book may be copied for congregational use.*

CONTENTS

10 2244

FIGURES

As you begin to read this book, you will be stepping into the presence of a wise and gentle teacher, a friend, a fellow-learner named John Ackerman. His first word of guidance is the same as his last and summarizes everything in between: *Give your entire attention to what God is doing right now.*

Learning how to attend to "what God is doing right now" is the lifelong work (and play) of the person of faith. Proficiency in attending to God is the source of all authentic ministry and the basis of spiritual authority. Helping people to attend to God—as individual souls and as faith communities—is the central work of the congregation.

At least in my lifetime and in the religious settings I have inhabited, ordained and lay leaders have generally found themselves unprepared for this central work. But we live in a graced moment. Ancient and contemporary wisdom about spiritual formation—springing from many different spiritual traditions, yet remarkably convergent in spirit—is available to any of us who is willing to seek, to knock, to ask.

For those who are already some distance along the learning path, this book will remind you of some truths you have already encountered, address some unanswered questions, and help you to bring it all down to earth in a living, breathing congregation. For those who are just beginning to seek guidance about the communal work of spiritual formation, this book will help you to plant your feet on a firm foundation.

It is hard for a book—a written form of speech—to convey a spirit of listening, but John Ackerman has somehow done it. Receptivity to living hearts and a living God pervade his conceptual frameworks, his stories, his guidance. Even in writing, John's "voice" models the gentleness, modesty, and openness required of anyone who would guide the spiritual formation of others. His tone invites us away from impatience, self-reproach, excessive concern with technique—to attend instead to the Mystery at the very center of our lives and our congregations. I hope and pray that you will accept this invitation!

ALICE MANN
Senior Consultant
The Alban Institute

W riting this book has been fun, a challenge, and hard work, depending on where in the process I have been. I've been comforted by the words of Winston Churchill: "Writing a book is an adventure. To begin with, it is a toy and an amusement; then it becomes a mistress, and then it becomes a master, and then a tyrant. The last phase is that just as you are about to be reconciled to your servitude, you kill the monster and fling him out to the public."

The toy and amusement stage was shared with the Christos Program for Congregational Leaders. We laughed a lot, especially about my proclivity for charts. I had fun reading books suggested by friends, particularly those suggested by Ed White. Jonna Fantz and Tom Allen helped design appendix A, on working on a mission statement, and Jonna wrote that part as well as appendix B, "Stop, Look, and Listen." My spiritual director continually encouraged me to be open to the Spirit as I wrote. I thank those whom I taught in doctor of ministry classes at Bethel Seminary, St. Paul, Minnesota; the classes at Columbia Seminary, Atlanta; Ghost Ranch in New Mexico; and Synod School in Iowa. They honed and clarified my thoughts. Eugene Peterson, Alice Mann, Howard Rice, and the Spiritual Formation Resource Team of the Presbyterian Church (U.S.A.) gave feedback on my early ideas. Our new dog Lili showed fine taste for devotional classics. She finds the English a bit dry, the Lutherans earthy, but is delighted to know that God is "dog" spelled backward.

The "mistress" part of writing was the romance of providing something useful for the church. The "master" part was having the idea accepted and a deadline set. My wife, Helen, commiserated with my moans as the computer lost chapters, and joined in my delight at stumbling over new insights and talking with everyone I could find, from fundamentalist to evangelical to mainline to New Age.

The cruel tyrant of writing was helped by Beth Gaede, tireless and fearless editor, dedicated to clarity at all costs. Jennie Bartholomew was very patient at collecting and designing my diagrams, and putting things in order. Jean Caffey Lyles polished and smoothed. I'm grateful that Ed White, Alice Mann, Tom Allen, and Vern Paul read the manuscript.

Instead of casting out a monster on the public, I regard this manuscript as an offspring. There are flaws, God knows. I only wish it could grow in dialogue with you, as my lectures do. But I am proud and pleased with the form this adventure has taken, and I hope that it will be helpful.

One note: I use the words "liberal," "evangelical," and "charismatic" simply as descriptive terms. Liberals could be called mainline. Evangelicals are conservatives, not fundamentalists. Charismatics generally stress the gifts of the Spirit.

"Today, if you hear his voice, do not harden your hearts" (Ps. 95:7b-8a). This admonition comes from both the Old and New Testaments. The call goes out to individuals and to the congregation (assembly). Jesus tells his disciples to listen, to pay attention. "Let anyone with ears listen" (Matt. 13:43).

It is my experience that few congregations listen to God's call to them, and few help members to listen to their individual call and to nurture their ongoing relationship with God. America is in the midst of a new spiritual revival, and many seekers are finding God outside congregations. People are hungry to know God in their own experience. But without a group to help, spiritual deformation will result.

Why this book? Because most congregations and people don't know how to listen to God. Congregations make up their minds by voting according to Robert's Rules of Order. They rarely listen to God or to each other. Individuals may be doing all kinds of work for God, but they rarely stop long enough to hear what God might have in mind. What would it be like for a wife to dote on her husband, cook him dinner, buy him neckties, dress up for him—but never ask what he likes?

What would it be like for a father to love his son, take him to ball games, play catch with him—but never ask the boy what he wanted to do? We say we love God or want to put God's will first in our lives; yet we never ask what God's desire is for our lives. *Listen.* ("Let anyone with ears listen" [Matt. 13:43]). By this I think Jesus meant us to notice God in our own immediate experience. Jesus wanted us to know God directly, not second-hand. Jesus meant that the disciples should discern God's voice in what Jesus was saying, and that together they would be led by the Holy Spirit to make decisions. Being led, filled, and guided by the Holy Spirit is the hallmark of the power of the New Testament church. Today secular theorists of adult education and organizational development have much to teach the church about the structure for listening.

Peter Drucker, pioneer management theorist, says, "Post-capitalist society has to be decentralized. Its organizations must be able to make fast decisions, based on closeness to performance."[1] Another theorist, Peter Vaill, author of management books, says that our culture is one of "permanent white water" (a continuing state of rapid change) and that leadership and teaching must be restyled. Donald Miller, researcher in contemporary religion, in a study of new congregations and what they have to say to traditional Protestant congregations, says: "Churches are mired in organizational structures that deaden vision as people gather endlessly in committee meetings."[2] He offers the heart of what I see as the opportunity for congregations: "*First*, they must give the ministry back to the people, which requires a flatter organizational structure. *Second*, they must become vehicles for people to access the sacred in profound and life-changing ways."[3]

The two mandates are interrelated. When there is a flatter organization structure, the individual has more responsibility. Experts can't provide all the answers for a person's soul. And when people do take more responsibility for their spiritual life, the congregation carries out a much more mutual ministry. The shape of our life together in communities helps form our individual spiritual lives. And our individual awareness of God's presence helps shape our common life. *Spirit at Work*, a book of essays by Parker Palmer and other writers on spirituality, includes a chart that I have adapted for my purposes:

Figure 1
Organizational Structure:
Hierarchy versus the Circle

STRUCTURE	HIERARCHY	CIRCULAR
Focus	Position	People
Outcome	Change	Transformation
Leadership Style	Domination Management	Partnership Collaboration
Spirituality	Dependent Oriented to others	Independent Inner-oriented to Spirit
Education	Experts tell Teacher-centered	God speaks Learner-centered

A movement from hierarchical to circular order is under way in many businesses. Churches should move in a similar direction if they are going to empower the laity. Churches need to learn to discern God's will in ways other than the majority will or what the experts say. Listening to God directly as a congregation moves the clergy from the role of expert and controller to that of facilitator and teacher. Then laypeople can exercise their own authority and are encouraged to listen to each other and to their own experience. This is not a simple or easy shift. In chapter 2, I show five areas in which a church might move in its development. The degree of circularity depends on the degree of growth.

What I offer in this book is my experience as pastor, teacher, and spiritual director, as well as my understanding of contemporary theory about the learning organization. I bring my experience as a pastor for 40 years, as a spiritual director for 20 years, and as a teacher of clergy for 10. I offer ways of looking at spiritual growth and suggest techniques that a church of any size can use to promote members' spiritual growth. The growing spirituality of members and especially leaders usually supports and encourages the health and growth of the congregation. One way to describe this book is to say that I offer tested ways of practicing spiritual discernment in ordinary congregations and for individuals. Discerning churches do not focus on denominational and seminary authority over the clergy and clergy authority over the laity, on the mind rather than the feelings and soul, on males rather than females and children, on old-timers rather than newcomers. Rather, these churches that empower people listen to newcomers, laity, women, and children and learn from them.

I believe God invites us to mutuality. Just as Jesus empowered others, we are being asked to do the same. I have found practices that nourish spiritual formation throughout the congregation for individuals and the whole. This book is not intended to inspire individual awareness alone or in small groups only. This book is not about leadership or clergy alone. This book is not about liturgy or sermons alone, but it is about the whole system, every-thing we do in a congregation to form us more fully into the body of Christ, and to become aware of Christ in us as members. I've discovered ways to make the connection between individual and community growth—mainly by trying approaches that didn't work!

LEARNING THE HARD WAY

I tried small groups, and most failed. I went to the Church of the Saviour, a pioneering church in Washington, D.C., made up of highly committed people in small groups practicing a journey inward (in spirituality), a journey out-ward (in social justice) and a journey together (in a small group). The people there nourished my spirit in spiritual direction and retreats, and influenced the way I run committees. They showed me the connection between spiri-tuality and social justice. But in all my years as a parish pastor, I have found only one small group in a large congregation that was willing to follow Church of the Saviour's model. While serving in other congregations I went to healing conferences and led healing services, and people stayed away in droves. I was trained as a spiritual director, but even in a very large church, people weren't interested. I invited Thomas Keating, a Trappist monk and popular speaker on spirituality, to teach "centering" prayer, and seven people of a congregation of 3,000 came. I introduced music from the French spiri-tual community Taizé and led *lectio divina* Bible study. I was fascinated by walking labyrinths to assist meditation. All these offerings failed to attract many people. I began to have qualms about encouraging the spiritual elite alone. I began to think that trickle-down spirituality didn't work. Focusing on those who like a new fad may only alienate further the rest of the congregation. Nourishing a small group of the like-minded didn't seem to benefit the whole congregation.

Pastors and churches are charged to minister to everyone, to all kinds of spiritual expression. I tried holding an all-church experience like the Roman Catholic program "Renew." In Renew, the church ceased all of its meetings for six weeks and sought to place every member in a small group. The pastor would preach about the theme the people were discussing. Some members gained much from small groups, but we were not able to close down meetings and to persuade all the leaders to get behind the program. In talking to Roman Catholics, I learned that the program wrought no permanent change in most congregations—except in those that formed ongoing groups led by facilitators who were continually guided by the pastor.

What did I learn from these wrong turns?

- The spiritual fad that appeals to me probably will not appeal to a large number of people. My agenda is often not the Spirit's agenda. What works for another parish probably will not work for my congregation.
- As a pastor, I need to serve the whole congregation as it is, and not as some imagined group. When I listened and received regular feedback about where people discerned God calling, we all grew. When I listened to people who were most different from me, I learned the most. What I learned the least from was success stories. Neighborhood people and my professional colleagues have helped me far more than a system that works for some successful preacher in suburbia.

I learned the most in the past 10 years from a little church that was dying. I thought my real ministry was not serving the congregation but practicing spiritual direction outside the congregation, facilitating four clergy support groups, and teaching "Spiritual Formation in the Congregation" in seminaries. This ministry seemed to be on the cutting edge, and I had a lot of energy for it. I had no enthusiasm or even a sense of call about this little church. I was mostly attracted to serve there because it helped pay my retirement package. The 15 people in this dying church were all over 60 years old. I thought the church would die in a few years. But as we prayed and listened, hope sprang up. We believed that we would be led. We were. I had to surrender my pessimistic viewpoint. Then we all had to give up our established agendas. I remember a congregational meeting struggling with the thought that if we were to grow, we would be changed. We were marvelously led by God to grow numerically and spiritually. These were the things we learned together:

- When people listen for God's leadership, direction is given. Direction came from people inside and outside the church. Guidance came from friends outside the system who affirmed our direction and told us that new people were moving into the neighborhood. Throughout the Bible, it is often the outsiders, not the insiders and professionals, who see best what God is doing.

- Spiritual formation takes place at the corporate, leadership, and individual levels. We had no permanent small groups that only prayed or specialized in spiritual formation. We got to know God in leadership meetings, in committees, in worship, and in the congregation as a whole. Sometimes we designed programs that touched the whole church. These included worship, small groups, and individuals. Sometimes we concentrated on helping individuals get in touch with God. It was easy to see how the whole Body of Christ worked in this one-cell church. Yet even here, the Spirit surprised us with new ideas and spiritual awareness in unexpected places and people. We began to notice signs of transformation or reformation. The church became alive, and individuals surrendered more deeply.

- It's good to have a mission statement that includes spiritual growth: It may make you wonder what "spiritual growth" is and whether you're doing it. Once we began placing new members in leadership positions, we wrote a statement. We were expressing a change in our culture. Our statement said that we would "develop personal relationships with God." We wondered together what spiritual formation would consist of. We started asking if we noticed the movement of the Spirit within the congregation and in individuals. We began evaluating ourselves by how well we were doing the tasks we thought God wanted us to do. Counting bodies or programs or dollars didn't necessarily give evidence of the Spirit.

- We decided that we needed to put God first, to see what God thought we were here for. Churches that are developing or redeveloping often say that spiritual energy must come before congregational and outreach development.

- It's important to learn from parishioners how they find God in the worship service. Liturgical experts and people in other congregations can't read the minds or hearts of your congregation. Book-learned theory can't replace the lived experience of worshipers. Every parish is unique. And it takes more than a questionnaire to listen. This listening is a continual process.

- A language that describes differences of spiritual style enables people to feel free to follow the path that is uniquely theirs. Tools describing spiritual styles or the Myers-Briggs Type Indicator provide a language that encourages differences. We found that knowing about differences led to accepting others and accepting our own style.[4]
- Road maps that describe individual and group development can tell you which ballpark you're in and what kind of game is being played. Otherwise you may think that one size fits all.
- We need to pay attention. This attending needs to start with the pastor and the leadership. Learning how to listen to God happens in worship and in committees and on occasions of helping people reflect on their experience. Corporately listening means becoming a learning community. Instead of following the lead of a great strategist at the top, everyone at every level learns and contributes. In the church it means that all members must learn how to listen to themselves, to others, and to the Holy Spirit, who animates all structures.

Again and again we found in the scriptures that God bids people pay attention. The introduction to the Shema, a prayer from scripture that Jews are commanded to say daily, says: "Hear, O Israel" (Deut. 6:4).

In Eugene H. Peterson's paraphrase of the Sermon on the Mount, Jesus says: "Give your entire attention to what God is doing right now" (Matt. 6:33 TM). Some older versions have it: "Seek ye first the kingdom of Heaven" (Matt. 6:33 KJV).[5]

Paul says in Romans: "Fix your attention on God" (Rom. 12:2 TM).

Hebrews says: "Take a hard look at Jesus. He's the centerpiece of everything we believe" (Heb. 3:1 TM).

"Today, please listen" (Heb. 3:15 TM).

I found that as I listened with the community, I was changed. Instead of relying on biblical commentaries for the answers, I started to notice what God was doing in our life together and to hear God speak daily in the Bible. I told more stories from my life, not just the big events, but also how I was being surprised by God in the ordinary times. The community members took more responsibility for their life together. I told more stories and quoted fewer books. Parishioners began to discover God in their own experience. The laypeople began to exercise leadership. There is a profound link between moving from hierarchical to circular leadership and the process whereby people find their own form of spirituality.

Once people know the Spirit within, they aren't about to cede a false authority to others. Once the pastor lets go of control, laypeople are empowered to lead, grow, and listen. I learned better how to mentor young leaders. I encouraged their spiritual development and leadership abilities. They taught me, or rather, we learned together how to become a team.

"Give your entire attention to what God is doing right now" (Matt. 6:33 TM). When I am asked what makes the difference between a congregation doing business as usual and one doing spiritual formation, I hope I remember to say "listening." Listening to God by the pastors, listening to God by the leaders, teaching leaders to listen to parishioners after worship, to outsiders hungering for good news, and to themselves. One way we listen to God is to pay attention to God in our experience.

If I learned anything as a pastor, it was to listen. It started with my listening to God in Scripture and my life, supported by a group and a spiritual guide. I started to listen to the congregation and to those outside the church. I helped form the new leaders with the experience of listening together, listening to newcomers, listening to worshipers, and listening in committees. Pretty soon listening became a set pattern for our life together, and the various parts became a system of listening that reinforced and informed all the parts.

As I started teaching other clergy in courses and coordinating four supervision groups, I discovered that I wanted to offer less intellectual content. Rather, I found what I had to share was exercises to help people listen to others, listen to God, listen to themselves. I remember one of my prize students pushing away her laptop computer during the first class session. I thought: "This class is going to be different." When students expected reading material, I found nothing in print that dealt with spirituality for leaders and congregations. I felt called to try to put our experience into print. Writing this book, teaching this material, and receiving feedback have also changed me. I've been noticing more clearly in retrospect where God was moving among us.

The practices we used are really very old. Wendy Miller, author and teacher of spiritual formation, offers a translation of Jesus responding to the question as to why he teaches in parables: "It's because you have a heart condition. Your inner ears are deaf, and the eyes of your spirit cannot see. Isaiah was right when he said: 'You will indeed listen, but never understand, and you will indeed look, but never perceive. For this people's heart has grown dull, and their ears are hard of hearing, and they have shut their eyes;

so that they might not look with their eyes, and listen with their heart and turn and I would heal them. But blessed are your eyes, for they see, and your ears, for they hear'" (Matt. 13:14-16).[6]

The mystery of God is hidden: it needs to be heard and seen in a new way. This mystery isn't limited to the spiritual elite, like the Gnostics in the early church, who thought they had a corner on God. The mystery of God is given to ordinary people who know God's Spirit in ordinary ways. An Olympic winner, a diver who overcame a broken foot and insufficient practice, was asked how she had won. She replied: "I can do all things through Christ." She spoke of visualizing herself doing her best, being present in the moment, filling her mind with the reality of her family. She knew the unseen mystery of Christ, God in her family, in her being in the moment. As Carolyn Gratton, one of my teachers at Duquesne University, writes: "Faith involves that radical transformation of perception that gives us the ability to see and understand something of this invisible reality that inheres in the visible."[7]

KNOWING

Paul Holmer, who taught philosophy at the University of Minnesota and at Yale Divinity School, made the distinction between knowledge or language *about* and knowledge or language *of*. Knowledge *about* is important. It is the language we use to build houses and shop for food and send e-mail and think about lots of things, including God. Language *of* is our response to life and God: it is the language often beyond words in joy, music, poetry, and spirituality. It is the language of listening and contemplation.

This knowledge of God is found in the mysterious, deep parts of Scripture that may not be intellectually understood but that speak to our hearts: "The Spirit prays in us with sighs too deep for words" (Rom. 8:26).

"Abide in me and I in you" (John 15:4). It is this language that I encourage here, although both kinds can bring us to God. As I read John Calvin, he encourages objective, theological thinking and subjective, led-by-the-Spirit knowing at the same time. Knowledge *about* and *of*, head knowledge and heart knowledge, join in a dance to and with God. I use this chart to make distinctions:

Figure 2
Three Ways of Knowing

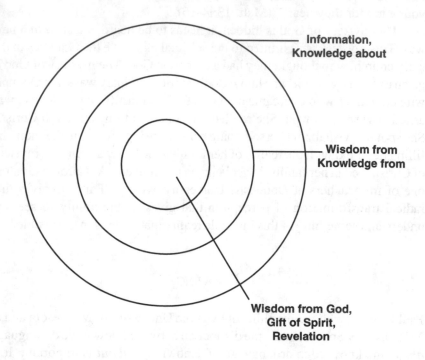

Information,
Knowledge about

Wisdom from
Knowledge from

Wisdom from God,
Gift of Spirit,
Revelation

Charts help me clarify my muddled thinking. They may help yours. Most of all I offer a series of exercises. Most of the things I talk about, like listening to God and each other, cannot be learned in a book or lecture. Doing these exercises is like riding a bicycle or driving a car. The ability to listen is a gift to be prayed for. It's also a skill that can be developed. The exercises can be adapted to your locality, your personality, your style. There is much more that could be said about congregational learning and individual listening, but in this book I have suggested the simplest, most elementary practices that help us begin to listen and learn. Remember; Jesus said that he would send the inner Teacher. This is experiential learning. These exercises may be thought of as a sanctuary, some space where we may change our pace and become aware of God's presence. Teaching a course for spiritual formation, Carolyn Gratton said: "A mystery like the indwelling of the spirit of Christ cannot be known except through the Spirit of God. Paul is telling us that we cannot figure out this type of wisdom or knowledge by ourselves."[8]

"But God hath revealed them unto us by his Spirit: for the Spirit searcheth all things, yea, the deep things of God" (1 Cor. 2:10 KJV).

"We didn't learn this by reading books or going to school; we learned it from God, who taught us person-to-person through Jesus, and we're passing it on to you in the same firsthand, personal way" (1 Cor. 2:13 TM).

Chapter 1

Laying a Foundation

There has been a sea change in the past 50 years in the nature and character of Christian spirituality. In the 1950s, spirituality was centered in churches. That was where one found God. Churches were organized with top-down authority. Scholars had more authority than laypeople, and the ordinary person in the pew found comfort in an institution. The tectonic shift has moved us from spirituality found in a place of dwelling to spirituality experienced in a group of seekers. According to Robert Wuthnow, sociologist and author of *After Heaven: Spirituality in America since the 1950s*, habitation spirituality focuses on the God who has a sacred space in heaven and on earth in which humans can dwell. Before the 1960s this belief was the predominant expression of spirituality in America. A "seeking spirituality," which arose in the 1960s, is characterized by knowing God on the journey rather than in houses of worship alone. In a "dwelling" spirituality, experts provide guidance for the laity, and a systematic way of thinking and behaving prevails. A seeking spirituality is focused not on a place so much as on the activity of searching for meaning, journeying through life. The new pattern accepts a great deal of diversity and choice. At its worst, it is a shopping-mall mentality; at best, searching acknowledges that one style of spirituality does not fit all. Characteristics of these two styles of spirituality tend to cluster as follows:[1]

HABITATION SPIRITUALITY	SEEKING SPIRITUALITY
A mighty fortress	Pilgrims in a barren land
Belonging	Choosing groups
Church: safe haven	Church: supplier of goods
We are alike	We are diverse yet one
Finding answers	Searching for meaning
My job in church is important	I choose to join a taskforce for a while

Both patterns are ancient and can be found in the Bible. Dwelling spirituality constructs the temple and finds God in the Holy of Holies; seeking spirituality is found in the desert, in the prophets. In *The Courage to Teach*, Quaker educator Parker Palmer, who has written extensively about education and spirituality, describes the shift in teaching styles. This change roughly parallels the shift in spirituality. In his chart below,[2] we see a top-down institutional approach to education and spirituality. Filters separate classes of people. The filters keep the material from backing up: there is no feedback. The object of study is "out there," the focus of scholarship. God as the object of study is "out there," working through priests, pastors, and teachers. They have gone to a special place of learning, and they read books; therefore, they are experts. The laypeople receive. In the second chart, the subject is in the midst of the community, and in the case of God, within people as well as among people. Mutual learning and mutual sharing result. This style is actually as old as the first, but it has been forgotten for several hundred years by the dominant culture of the Western world. It is the consensus model, used by Eastern Orthodox, Native American, and Quaker communities.

Figure 3
The Objectivist Myth of Knowing

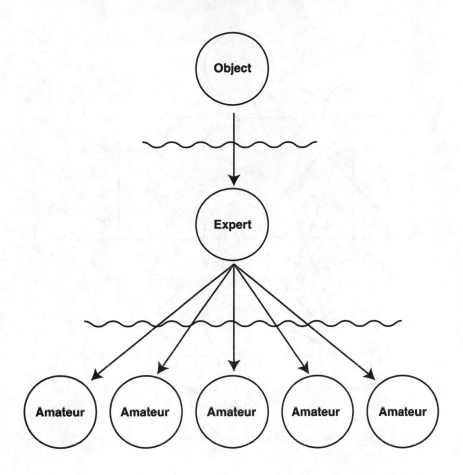

Figure 4
The Community of Truth

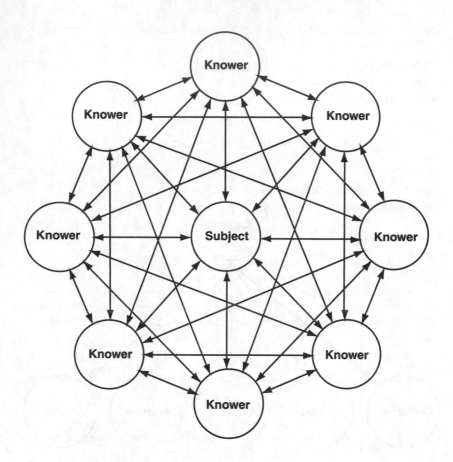

When I was growing up, I never heard the word "spirituality." There were devotional books for daily prayer, and if someone wanted to find God, he or she went to a church. Devotion was connected to church, for God was assumed to be best known inside churches.

When I asked my pastor for a book on prayer, he gave me a large book that analyzed different kinds of prayer. First there should be adoration and then confession and then other kinds. Learning to pray this way felt like learning where my feet should go in a waltz, but missing out on the music. In a library or bookstore, I would have been hard-pressed to find a book on the spiritual life. Since my boyhood days, big changes have taken place. One-third of baby boomers have dropped out of church. But the evangelical and charismatic churches are growing. They offer spirituality for seekers, worship where one can experience God. Interest in spirituality is found both inside and outside the church.

Recent years have seen an exponential increase in books that may be labeled "New Age" or "inspirational." People are fascinated by spiritual growth, and many turn to groups outside the church to find it. Churches that help provide people a religious experience are experiencing membership growth, especially those churches with programs for discipleship.

Spirituality is not designed to enhance our egos primarily. (Let your prayers be in secret so your Father who sees in secret may reward you.) There is a reward: the fruit is joy, peace, love.

But there are styles in Christian religion today.[3]

Figure 5
Three Contemporary Religious Styles

	Old Style	Emerging New	New Age
Who has the responsibility for spiritual growth?	The hierarchy, the professors, the authors	The local congregation	The individual
Who is the authority?	The experts	Our common life	Me
How does spiritual formation take place?	Sacraments, worship, study	Listening to God, obeying, being in community	Pick and choose
Prayer	Done by experts, taught by experts	God teaches, the community teaches	Everything is prayer
Spirituality	Dwelling	Journeying together	Seeking
Leaders are credentialed	Academic preparation	Spiritual experience,	Experts in the field

It may be useful to draw some distinctions among different expressions and styles in religion. Admittedly, the chart above simplifies the reality of the religious scene today. I see, for instance, in the Roman Catholic Church that the hierarchy retains the old style, that some spiritual directors and congregations are solidly into the new style, and that some retreat centers appear to be New Age.

The churches in column 2 are, by and large, growing. The old-style churches in the first column are declining. The third column, "New Age," is rapidly expanding. Browse at any large bookstore, and you'll likely find a "New Age" section—including volumes on self-help, holistic practices, the blending of world religions (often drawing on Eastern or American Indian traditions); and concern for nature, spirituality, or the supernatural. I think that the growing edge in American churches is in column 2. It is for column 2 congregations that I write. I suggest that:

1.   The emerging new American churches are places where responsibility for spiritual growth is not up to the clergy or experts like spiritual directors, but rather the whole congregation.

2.   The authority for the church is our communal listening to the Spirit of the risen Christ, the Spirit within and among us.

3.   Formation doesn't just happen by having the right theology or liturgy. Spiritual formation happens when individuals and congregations together can listen to God, obey God, and be transformed by God.

4.   Despite our pitiful attempts to have someone else do our praying for us, or to teach us the right way to do it, the Spirit of God is the "inner teacher" and is teaching us.

5.   Some people find it comfortable to be part of a congregation that gives answers and instructions. Others prefer being on a perpetual search. Many are finding that they want to hear God calling them to a spiritual journey in the good company of other disciples.

6.   While academic preparation is important, more and more congregations are looking for leaders who continue to learn, who know how to assist the learning of others, who are accountable in their ministry and spiritual practice, and who have sound character.

THE MEANING OF SPIRITUALITY

For me the word "spirituality" is identical to what the old word "mystical" suggested: an experience of God. A classic expression of this concept is found in the story of Job, who said, "I admit I once lived by rumors of you; now I have it all firsthand—from my own eyes and ears!" (Job 42:5 TM). Spirituality means roughly the same thing that piety meant to reformers John Calvin and Martin Luther: reverence toward God, listening to God. Both Luther and Calvin had a lively sense of the Holy Spirit as the teacher within, the initiator of prayer and good works. Sanctification is God's work in us. One of Luther's favorite ideas was that we listen to God and God listens within us. Piety is of the heart more than the head, or rather the mind *in* the heart, as Calvin said. Luther said that we could pray with our minds, but when the Spirit came with rich, warm thoughts, we should let our mind give way. I would add that the biblical understanding of spirituality involves our neighbors and ourselves. The biblical summary is: "You shall love the Lord your God with all your heart, and with all your soul, mind, and strength, and you shall love your neighbor as yourself" (Mark 12:29).

Spirituality is the opposite of knowing *about* God with our reason and stopping there. Spirituality does not stop with accepting dogma about God, reading the Bible with our mind and understanding principles, making a comparative study of religion and developing a philosophy. Some commentators say that spiritual knowledge of God is intuitive, affective. Spirituality is generically understood as the search for meaning, finding something greater than oneself to belong to.

Christian spirituality is grounded in Jesus Christ. Christian spirituality is formed by Christ's life, teaching, death, resurrection, and presence in the heart of the believer and in the body of Christ, the church. It might be called "the spiritual life." Christian spirituality is concerned that people are formed into Christ. "Little children, for whom I am again in the pain of childbirth, until Christ is formed in you" (Gal. 4:19).

Forming is the beginning, and transforming is the goal—the goal is that Christ, and not our egos, be at the center of our lives. Christian spirituality takes the form of the cross: a surrender to Christ, who has laid down his life for us. Christians who seek to grow spiritually listen to the risen Christ in scripture and in life, and obey the call of God. Spirituality is not designed to enhance our egos. The focus is on God. Our ego is superficially the center of our personality. But in faith we know the presence of our soul or spirit.

We were created in the image of God, and that image is never completely erased. That image of God may become the center of our life more and more as we surrender to God, and as Christ dwells in our hearts by faith. Our ego is not destroyed but reconfigured, recentered, remade.

SPIRITUALITY AND RELIGION

At first it seems as though the modern culture is right. The spiritual life seems to differ from religion in several ways. In common understanding, popularly expressed, here are the differences:

Figure 6

RELIGION	SPIRITUALITY
Knowledge about God	Knowledge of God
Reading, ideas, fixed	Practice, searching, mystery
Studying the Bible	Hearing God address me in the Bible
Controlling my life	Being led by the Spirit
Knowing about religions	Seeing God as mystery
Relying on reason alone	Relying on God
Our work	God's work
Our spiritual growth	God's agenda for me and my growth

But that is an either/or view of reality. The great Christian writer Baron Friedrich von Hügel suggested that religion has three parts.[4] I have taken his three elements and added the charge that Jesus gave to his church, "Go, and make disciples of all nations, baptizing them in the name of the Father, Son, and the Holy Spirit, teaching them to observe all that I have commanded you" (Matt.28:19-20).

Figure 7
Von Hügel's Three Elements of Religion

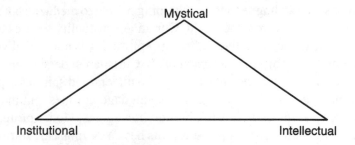

Mystical

Institutional   Intellectual

It seems to me that this is a balanced view, and every congregation and individual should have all three in working order. Von Hügel thinks that we start off as children in the institutional church. This experience is external, what Mommy and Daddy and the church say, historical and traditional. This stage may be heartfelt, lasting all of life. But later, in adolescence, children learn to think critically and scientifically. The third part of religion moves people to action, to find one's real self, the deeper personality. People want experiential religion, mysticism.

Most denominations and congregations and individuals are unbalanced, says von Hügel. They emphasize one aspect to the detriment of the others. Von Hügel practiced spiritual direction by correcting the imbalance of individuals. For example, when Evelyn Underhill, English author of *The Study of Mysticism*, first asked him to be her spiritual director, she was already a well-known author of spiritual books. Von Hügel said that her religion was overintellectualized. She needed to cut out some of the social and intellectual visits with friends and serve the poor each week. She should to go to mass weekly. She later said that her religion up to that point had been vague and unfocused. At the end of six months, Christ was real to Underhill, and her spiritual practices were oriented toward him and down to earth.

The church I grew up in was all intellectual and institutional. So were my seminary and most of the seminaries I have known. My bias for the past 20 years has been to find God in the mystical and intellectual and not particularly in the institutional. Now God seems to beckon me back into a balance of finding God in the ordinary and the institutional aspect of the church. I see this pattern with individuals and churches. Religious health calls for a balance.

Along with the bias that separates spirituality from religion, other misunderstandings persist: Christian spirituality is not spiritualism. Spiritualism
most often is known by seances—efforts to talk to the dead. Spiritualism
often emphasizes healing services and helping people to meditate, but many
times it seems cut off from the world. Christian spirituality focuses on the
living Lord, incarnate in our lives. Christian spirituality is not spirit divorced
from body and life. This is a perversion of the Christian understanding. This
attitude goes back to the ancient Greeks, who understood spirit as separate
from the material world. Paul speaks this language at times, but the flesh
for Paul isn't just material; it is life in rebellion against God. Spiritual life
isn't against fun or the body or pleasure at its best. Yes, monastic spirituality
and the Puritans often sound that note. But the full Christian understanding
of the spiritual life is life in community, unity of the body, mind, and spirit,
with love and laughter. Spirituality is often seen as a threat. My experience
with every denomination or theological perspective is that new practices
are seen as coming from the enemy camp. Maybe all of us are afraid of the
perversions of spirituality we have seen. Perhaps we project our fears of
otherness onto our journey with God.

MODERN DEVELOPMENT OF SPIRITUALITY IN AMERICA

What has happened since the 1950s?[5] Alcoholics Anonymous came of age
and influenced 50 million Americans, and separated spirituality from religion as never before. It started as a group in church basements, where
personal stories of hell and redemption were told each week. People surrendered again and again to God or a "Higher Power." People admitted
their real sins rather than making a corporate confession that encouraged
no self-examination. People made amends, spoke to God, listened to God,
and looked for God in their lives. People were transformed.

Buddhism and Zen taught meditation instead of a solely intellectual
faith. Returning Vietnam veterans and intellectuals found that they more
easily gained access to dogma-free Eastern spirituality. And the Eastern
religions taught methods of prayer and meditation that the Western church
had forgotten. Many Christians began talking to their counterparts of other
faiths. Thomas Merton, 20th-century monk and writer on spirituality, re-
ported that Eastern monks were far more advanced in techniques of
meditation. People found that there were more choices than Protestant,

Catholic, and Jew. Some Christians fled into stricter orthodoxy, while many went to the other extreme. I know of many Christians who go to church regularly, attend a Zen or Yoga center, and read books written by an Islamic poet. That can be all right if one has a clear sense of accountability to a group, clearness in theology, and boundaries in practice.

Business learned the necessity of reducing the bureaucracy, of moving away from an authoritarian model where only the CEO learned. This trend has affected the church's models of organization. Some have estimated that the church bureaucracy is about 10 years behind business in its structure. Now in business schools and in practice, efforts focus on transformation into a learning organization with decentralized power. Authors of business books often teach the church how to empower members, become a learning organization, and differentiate between authority and leadership, between leadership and management. My experience is that in many communities one sees cross-fertilization of practices and ideas among business executives, psychologists, spiritual directors, and teachers. Some in teaching have changed their image of what teaching is all about, and this attitude is spilling over into the church. In the 1970s the liberation theologians found that academically oriented teaching oppressed its recipients. Then teachers discovered that straight-line, rational thinking alone was no longer demanded by much of the world. Businesses and researchers wanted people who could do "systems thinking," who could look at the whole.

Physics changed from a Newtonian view of the world, or mechanical certainty, to the mystery found in the expanding universe and the inner dance in the atom. Relativity and uncertainty and new discoveries destroyed much of the myth of scientific certainty and objectivity. Some scientists talked of God and said there was a place for religion and spirituality.

Postmodernism

Many call the present stage of thought "postmodern." They usually mean that the point of view our culture has maintained for the past 200 years has shifted. No longer do we insist on the rationality that we have sought since the time of the Enlightenment. Now we see a place for nonrational subjectivity, and we question whether objective truth exists. Since most theology in our culture has been rationalistic, this shift makes a big difference in thinking about God and worship and spirituality. Thinkers schooled by the

Enlightenment had a bias against tradition and insisted that people could think for themselves. Reason alone was enshrined.

Postmodernism goes further, to say that everything is ad hoc, everything is "virtual reality." The good part of this hypothesis is the recognition that no one group, especially "dead white males," defines reality. All knowledge depends on our perspective, and no one view can explain everything. Above all, no one system is innocent of error; our ego and need for power influence our intellectual comprehension. The younger generations come to church with different expectations about the reality of God, the truth of Scripture, the objectivity of theology. Doug Bannister, pastor and author, tells a joke illuminating this movement: Three umpires are having a Coke after a baseball game. One says, "There's balls and there's strikes, and I call 'em the way they are." Another responds, "There's balls and there's strikes, and I call 'em the way I see 'em." The third umpire says, "There's balls and there's strikes and they ain't nothing until I call 'em."[6]

I grew up in the world of objectivity with the first umpire. My children grew up in the world of the second umpire, and today's adolescents are growing up with the world of the third umpire. There is no fixed truth, only what we call truth. This approach can lead to complete skepticism and relativism on the negative side. More positively, this subjectivity can lead to humility and learning from others and may motivate us to continue to listen to God.

Worship and Spiritual Growth

In his introduction to the book of Revelation, Eugene Peterson, a translator and paraphraser of the New Testament, writes: "[John] is responsible for a circuit of churches on the mainland whose primary task is worship. Worship shapes the human community in response to the living God. If worship is neglected or perverted, our communities fall into chaos or under tyranny."[7]

The most important way that we become formed into Christ is in worship. It is in the ordinary congregation, warts and all, that most Christians most of the time have found God and become transformed. It is finally through singing unsingable hymns, loving irritating neighbors, listening to boring sermons and receiving clumsily administered sacraments that we are formed into the body of Christ and Christ is formed in us. It is in praising God in community that we become ourselves. It is in the family of

God that we are remade. The congregation itself is the guru, the dispeller of darkness.

Sermons that are preached from the center, experience, the heart and head, that are passionate with God's love, speak to our minds and hearts. The sacraments move past our minds to a deeper kind of knowing. We enter into the reality of God, the Trinity. The Trinity says something about God and something about us. God is community, yet with individual persons. The Father is not the Son, and the Son is not the Spirit. But all are one. There is unity and diversity. We hardly ever experience this paradox of knowing. We know how to be individuals, and we know how to be in community, but we don't know how to be communities of individuals. Individuality easily becomes loneliness, and community easily becomes a fusion of people. Only when we are fully mature do we know interdependence. For Christians, the Trinity is the primary symbol of a community that holds together by containing diversity within itself.

Many of my friends have trouble with the doctrine of the Trinity. It was formed by the early church to safeguard the mystery of who we believe God is. I remember teaching about the Trinity in my first pastorate with a chart that looked like a plumbing diagram. No one got very excited, but I had done my duty. Recently I read again a view of the Trinity by Brother David Steindl-Rast, a Benedictine monk who writes:

> Gratefulness is simply one way of experiencing the life of the Triune God within us. The life springs forth from the Father, the fountain and wellspring of divinity, the ultimate Giver. The total self-gift of the Father is the Son. The Son receives everything from the Father and becomes the turning point in this giving. For in the Holy Spirit the Son returns to the Father's ultimate giving as ultimate thanksgiving. The Triune God is Giver, Gift, and Thanksgiving. This movement from the Father through the Son in the Spirit is what St. Gregory of Nyssa called "the round dance of the Blessed Trinity." This is how God prays: by dancing.[8]

I think this nonhierarchical view of God may appeal to some feminists. Perhaps we can add feminine figures to the circle of God's community.

The view of God as dancing leads me to delight. It seems akin to modern systems theory, and allows for images and mystery, thinking and feeling. God is community, and we are invited to join the community and dance. The Father is not the Son, who is not the Holy Spirit: we may keep our identity and yet live in intimate love. For men struggling for intimacy and women struggling for individual identity, this is good news. So our worship might reflect the God we focus on, by helping us join the dance. Good liturgy helps us praise God with out bodies and hearts and minds. Worship is a primary way of being formed, shaped, oriented, as the people of God.

Prayer

What makes worship especially vital is the complementary movement of the daily prayer of individuals. Prayer includes everything from begging to praise to thanksgiving to meditation to contemplation. Certain varieties of prayer fit certain personalities; various forms of prayer are used for different times of life. Some people are attracted to thinking prayer, while others want to involve the heart or the body. Some want written prayers; others insist that their prayer be spontaneous. We often outgrow the prayer of childhood, only to rediscover childlike prayers in maturity.

A critical point in our spiritual growth is waking up spiritually. Most of us are asleep most of the time, unaware of God's presence. We read the Bible and may get the sense of it but miss the Living Lord. We go to church, and we hear no word to obey, nothing to change. We pray and fail to listen for the response. All through the Bible we read calls to listen, to watch, to pay attention. When we pay attention, we are aware that we have been asleep. A friend recently said, "God has been giving me wake-up calls, but I've been hitting the snooze button." And when we wake up, we may know that we are not in charge, that we are invited to mystery. According to the writer Frederick Buechner, "There is no event so commonplace but that God is in it, always hiddenly. Listen to your life. See it for the fathomless mystery that it is."[9]

Whether spiritual growth flowers depends on one's reaction to God, and that reaction depends partially on our community. As my congregation encouraged people to tell their stories, I found that frequently listeners could identify a similar moment in their own lives. ("Oh, you mean that that was God? I thought it was just a weird moment.") The community helps us not to run away from our awareness of God, to stay awake.

A significant moment occurs when prayer becomes a mutual relationship. Very simply, this exchange may start with our saying thank you for gifts given. Conversational prayer may develop. Many people are afraid of listening to God because the voice of God seems to them only an act of the imagination. How do we know our dialogue is with God? Because other people confirm its rightness, and the message sounds like God, because our lives are changed so we become more loving.

I believe that prayer is listening to God in scripture and life. How can you do the will of God until you hear it spoken to you? How can you know the spiritual discipline to which God is inviting you unless you ask?

Listening Spirituality

Patricia Loring, a Quaker, is the author of *Listening Spirituality*. She describes this spirituality thus:

> By listening I mean the widest prayerful, discerning attentiveness to the Source intimated within us, evidenced through others, and discernible through the experiences of life. This kind of listening is not only auditory. It may be visual, kinesthetic, intuitive or visceral as well, depending on the deepest attentiveness natural to the particular person.[10]

This attentiveness, this attitude of paying attention, seems to be what Jesus taught his disciples as primary, and what is lacking in many Christians today. We have been taught to listen to an expert standing in the pulpit or at the lectern, or writing in a book, so that we are not encouraged to trust our own discernment of experience. Spiritual disciplines are meant to help us listen at every level to God. The worship of the community and our listening prayer are the two focal points for spiritual formation.

Exercises

1. How do you define spirituality and religion? How do they interrelate in your parish?

2. Where were the hints of God in your individual and community history: wonder, passion, longing, belonging, truth, compassion for others? Can you add others?

Chapter 2

Maps of the Country

I like to look at maps. Especially when I'm lost they help show the way home. C. S. Lewis, English author of popular theology and children's books, said that creeds and theology are like maps: they are not the thing itself, but an abstraction that may show relationships. Here are "maps" that I use for congregations and individuals.

1. Congregations are not all alike in their way of listening to God. We make serious mistakes in teaching spiritual formation unless we know the climate of a congregation.
2. We change as individuals in the way we relate to God and to each other. Stage theory—the concept that people grow through distinct intervals of psychological or spiritual change—can help us accept where we are and give us some clues about what happens in transitions. Stage theory may help us understand other people better.
3. At its best, stage theory gives us a general map of what it means to make disciples, to encourage spiritual formation on the part of individuals and community.

There are many kinds of maps of individual spirituality stages: in the early church, these were thought of as stair-stepped on a ladder. Some people were more advanced than others. Theresa of Avila—Medieval mystic, teacher, and spiritual guide—thought of the stages as rooms in an interior castle. Some Protestants thought of the stages as justification, sanctification, and glorification. I have trouble trying to sort out spirituality as such, or grading stages of prayer. These systems seem to say that if we only try harder, we'll be closer to God. Nevertheless, there are differences. We can think of the spiritual life as a journey, and some people are farther along because of their experience. But unlike the stages of physical maturation, the stages of spiritual or psychological maturity don't always happen naturally. People may be slowed down because they have been abused, or because they have a limiting view of God. The congregational setting can help keep people stuck or can encourage growth.[1]

One map of spiritual growth that I find helpful includes the story of the disciples as a metaphor, a story about relationships, that may help congregations and individuals to diagnose where they are. Chart 1 is a description of emotional and character maturity, stages of loving. This is not exactly the same as spiritual stages, although the psychological maturity aspect forms the base for the spiritual. I think of the spiritual relating to the psychological as the wine relates to the cup. The psyche is the container for the spirit: it shapes the soul. Most of the time, spiritual maturity depends on emotional and character development.

EXAMINING THE STAGES

We are usually in a "home stage," but we can regress quickly because of shame, or function at a more sophisticated level when we are with a group that causes us to grow. We often need help moving from one stage to another. We become stuck when God and life are inviting us to the next stage and we refuse. Here are the stages in order of development, with a general description first, and then an illustration from the experience of the disciples:

Stage 1. Dependent. We develop basic trust, and naturally have a sense of wonder and openness toward the world. The world is filled with magic and fantasy; we have imaginary playmates. Santa is real; God may be known viscerally, and then in the imagination. At this stage we are dependent on others. We can't earn money, prepare our food, or take care of ourselves. We are psychologically dependent on others also. Without people to hold us, we shrivel up and die (like babies in understaffed orphanages in war-torn countries). Children may have vivid experiences of God, and new curricula help encourage their natural sense of wonder. Imagine the disciples at this stage. They learned their goodnight prayers and the 31st Psalm at their mother's knee. They prayed three times a day with family and community. They learned certain parts of scripture by heart. They knew they were dependent on God for everything.

Stage 2. Counterdependence. We form a new identity by leaving father and mother and becoming part of a group. As a group, we realize that we are different from others. It is "us against them"—us against, different from, our parents. We fight our dependence to have a voice of our own, to find a new identity as a member of a new group. During this period the disciples met Jesus, who called them to be followers and disciples. Jesus disciplined them by their common life and by teaching them to see God in a new way. They competed like adolescents to be the closest, the first.

Stage 3. Mutual Dependence. We learn to grow up and take a job and become responsible. We have a sense of duty and belonging; we can sacrifice for the greater good, for the future. We can accept group discipline and can discipline ourselves. We believe in the rule of law, which is greater than our leaders. There remains a hierarchy of dependence. The preacher needs the positive acclaim of the congregation. The husband needs the affection of his wife, and the wife depends on her husband. There is a natural codependency that is unhealthy, since neither husband or wife is really a whole self, and neither leader nor group can exist without the other. The disciples became mature and were sent out two by two to preach and heal. They became apostles. Jesus said he was going to Jerusalem and that he would no longer be with them in the flesh but would send the Spirit, the Friend. No longer were they servants, but friends. Stage 3 ended abruptly, and they reverted to stage 1 when they all fled at the time of the crucifixion. When life comes tumbling in, we can regress to earlier stages or we may hear God inviting us into the darkness, into the next step.

Stage 4. Independence. We learn that we are alone and in the dark at times. We begin developing a fragile inner authority and can accept responsibility for our failures. God may be eclipsed, and we are in the dark—at least in the old ways of knowing God. The disciples returned to the upper room and prayed and waited. They faced their guilt and despair. They wondered whether God had forsaken them.

Stage 5. Interdependence. We are able to be in community in a new way, as truly ourselves, with God in the midst. God is in us and in others and in us together. We are given a unitive glimpse, and our love matures. God is in all things, and we are prayed through. Pentecost came, and the disciples knew God in a new way, inside them and among them. They had found a new way of knowing God. God revealed himself in a new way. It took several centuries for the church to put this experience into theological form in the doctrine of the Trinity.

Figure 8
Chart 1: Growth Stages

1	2	3	4	5
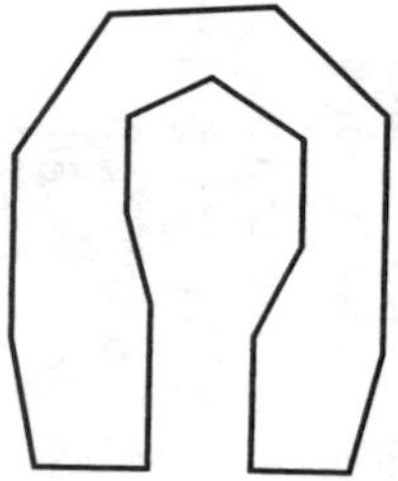 **Dependence**	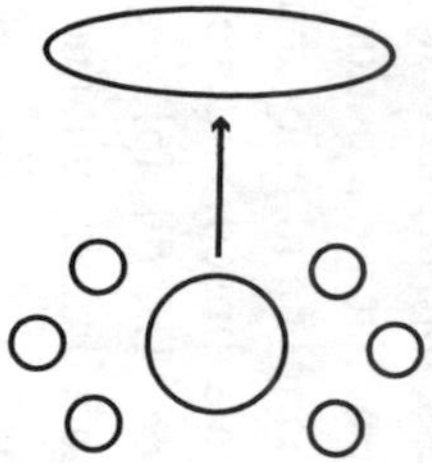 **Counter-Dependence**	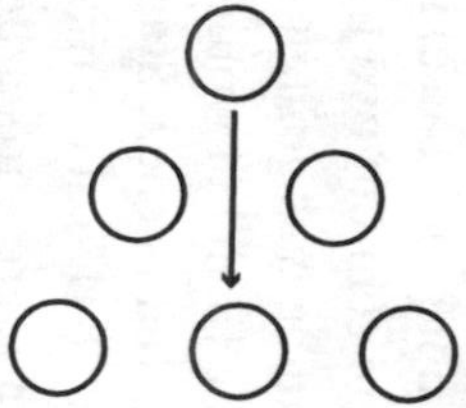 **Mutual Dependence**	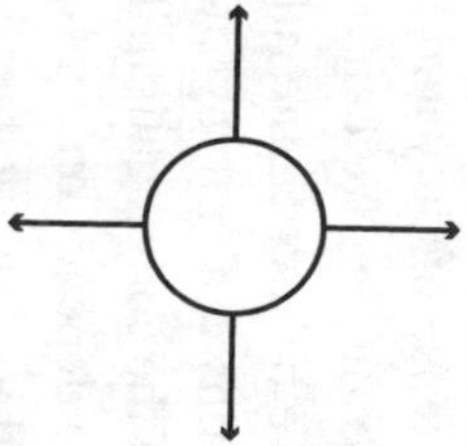 **Independence**	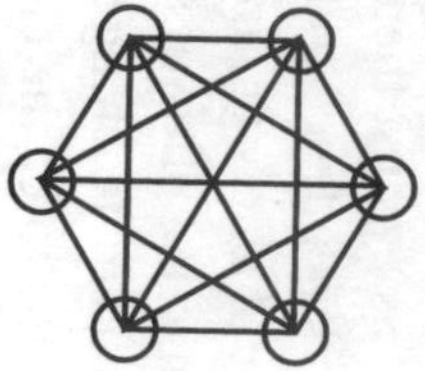 **Interdependence**
We are in our mother's womb, then in the womb of the family. We are dependent.	We are against something—parents the enemy—and form a gang. We are counter-dependent.	We become part of a group with a hierarchy, principles. We are mutually dependent or conventional.	We become independent; our meaning comes from within.	We become interdependent; and are able to keep our center in God while affirming God in others.

Figure 9
Chart 2: Growth of Community

	1. Dependence	2. Counterdependence	3. Mutual Dependence	4. Independence	5. Interdependence
Jesus & Disciples	Jesus' call	Arguments, rivalry	Disciples are mature	Jesus leaves, emptiness	The Spirit comes
Our experience	Wonderful excitement	Whose will is supreme?	We have bylaws, tradition, scripture	God may be calling in the darkness	Christ is in me. We are the Body of Christ
God's self revelation	Honeymoon Will you give thanks?	Ego willfulness vs God's will	The Kingdom	Why have you forsaken me?	Abide in me, I in you. It seemed good to the Holy Spirit and us.
Salvation	Belonging	Deliverance	Being justified	Reconciliation	Working with others and God

These build on each other and we go back and forth. The most important thing is the vertical dimension and where God is at each stage.

Look at chart 1. Does this represent to some extent the story of the Disciples? What does chart 2 say about your own experience? Where do you think you are right now? Where is your church right now?

Figure 10
Chart 3: Steps for Individual Leaders

	1. Dependence	2. Counter- dependence	3. Mutual Dependence	4. Independence	5. Inter- dependence
	Awakening to God	Struggle: whose way?	Conventional discipline, discipleship	Darkness, unknowing	Communion, union
Prayer	Help! You are great!	Deliver from enemies!	Send me your law; show me your light	Be with me in my doubt. Why have you forsaken me?	You; you are in the hearts of strangers
Need to grow	Develop skills of praying, listening	Find a sponsor or mentor, get feedback from group	Be alone, tolerate silence	Let go of resentment, self- pity, find God in all things	Mentor others
Leaders need to facilitate	Help from family	Have a cause, learn rules	Find clarity in mission, develop inner community life	Face your own and corporate shadow	Decentralize, use consensus, be flexible
Leaders need to lead individuals	Personal power from God	Inspire trusts & dependency	Inspire winning attitude	Inspire hope, integrity.	Empower, inspire love and service

Where are the leaders in your congregation? This is a critical issue. Take a look at chart 3. I have borrowed much of this material from *Real Power*, by Janet Hagberg, who has written extensively on leaders' growth and leadership style. This chart includes suggestions for growing. Leaders are called to be pacers, mentors, living the new reality of more intimacy with God.

What about hints for individuals and congregations at various stages? Here is a brief summary.

Stage 1. Children and wounded adults are often at this stage. The task developmentally is to establish trust, to encourage wonder and intimacy with people and with God. Little children in "good-enough" families do this naturally. The thinking behind this approach is that children naturally know God through their wonder. Instead of pumping them full of Bible verses, we can help evoke their sense of mystery as they hear the Bible stories. We can help them establish rituals in their homes, as described in *To Dance with God*, by Gertrude Mueller Nelson, a Jungian psychologist who writes about family rituals. I have seen some of this approach taught with joy and laughter, and I have seen some taught with deadly seriousness. I'd go for the laughter myself. I'd also notice children who seem naturally open to the divine mystery in nature. Many people have told me that their experience of looking at ants or beetles suddenly made them aware that a larger presence was looking at them.

A host of wounded adults cannot relate to the church naturally because God has been introduced as part of an abusive system of guilt and shame. God for them is a monster who killed his son, and who wants to devour them.

Wounded people and nations are susceptible to charismatic leaders like Adolf Hitler and founders of religious cults. Healing for these wounded people can take place partly in churches that hold healing services, sponsor 12-step ministries, practice laying on of hands, and encourage healthy spiritual formation. I have attended several charismatic churches whose healing ministries don't keep people dependent forever. Good healers help the wounded grow into spiritual maturity.

In summary, children at this stage are natural listeners who need to be encouraged. Wounded people also know the dark side of religion and family. They need help to establish trust, find healing, and move past their wounds. Congregations at this stage need tender loving care. They most likely need mature, loving pastors and leaders for those who have been abused, leaders who can help them be healed from the abuse of clergy or others who betrayed their trust. In Georges Bernanos's novel *The Diary of a Country Priest*, the story of a Roman Catholic cleric in France, one character suggests that the church has it all wrong. We start beginners out in small churches, and clergy work their way up to be administrators or bishops. The character suggests that maybe it ought to be the other way around, so that we send the most mature to the small, unloved parishes, and put young seminarians in office-based administrative positions. When I suggest this notion to mature clergy who have served badly hurt congregations, they enthusiastically agree. The kind of learning that takes place in congregations at this stage may be largely nonverbal. It's the love of a leader that is communicated at this and every level, and the words are secondary in importance. We all need love, and one of the delights in church is that we may be sung to, read to, touched, and loved in the name of a Father and Mother who will not take advantage of us.

Stage 2. These people are seen most typically as adolescents, though many grown men particularly never leave this stage. Most adventure movies have stage 2 heroes or heroines. They are forever taking justice into their own hands, fighting evil, creating an empire, or making piles of money. People who have become addicted to drugs in adolescence are usually at stage 2. Parishioners here develop their doubt and intellect. They may be highly skeptical of church and parents. Children from liberal families may be attracted to evangelical or "new paradigm" churches. Those in conservative groups may become more liberal. This is a time for romance and for romantic leaders. Those who follow a quest will be diligent in following their passion, whether the quest be in technology, ministry, or spirituality. Adolescents form new peer groups, a new family, and find much of their energy in fighting authorities. Devoting ourselves to a cause or group greater than ourselves is exciting and sets us on our way.

The darker side of this stage can be seen when the competition—appropriate in sports—comes into school and business and church. It may be difficult to guide young men and women to form teams and cooperate if the final score, the grade, is always individualistic. Young people who enter business may be competitive and successful, and yet driven and lonely. Many successful clergy I know are driven entrepreneurs who are in this stage. They are highly competitive, lonely, and often tempted by the adolescent triad of wine, women, and song (well, maybe song is all right).

Learning to listen at this stage may be listening to Jesus, the hero, the one who beckons, but it may be perverted into an orientation toward success. Many of the success stories of big churches say in effect, "Follow Jesus this way, and you'll have big churches." Congregations at this stage are often dysfunctional and split into factions. The spirituality committee may become just one more contested turf, wanting money and time and people. There is little real learning for a congregation stuck in stage 2 until someone exerts enough power to set boundaries, remind people of church rules, and tell leaders who makes decisions about what. (The treasurer doesn't make financial policy; the governing board has that power). The successful interim pastors I have known are able to exercise this kind of strong leadership well. Pastors with stage 2 churches can work with a group to develop a mission statement that is greater than any individual agenda. This kind of church needs strong leadership. Unfortunately it usually gets a new pastor right out of seminary, or one who has no congregational support, and the church becomes one in a line of failures.

Evangelicals call forms of leadership development at this stage "discipling." These patterns have been developed for high school and college students. The student groups InterVarsity and Navigators are the ones

I know best. They stress scripture study, accountability for behavior, and intercessory prayer. Evangelicals are usually strong on disciplines and character formation, but in my experience they apparently have no stage development beyond stage 3. Mainline programs seem to be written for stage 4—which is probably where the curriculum writers are. But when young "liberal" adults are in church, they need disciplines and accountability.

Stage 3. Our culture calls this stage adulthood. Indeed, 60 percent of the American population does not go beyond this stage. Spirituality focuses on belonging, making commitments, doing one's duty. Commitments are made to the status quo, to hierarchical authorities. Leaders at this stage need to control. And congregations expect them to. They are dependent on leaders to say what's right, what should be believed, how to pray. Church members don't want to be open to the spirit within them, their own autonomy.

Teachers need to be expert and credentialed. Congregations and pastors want success. Stage 3 folk are buying into the myths of our society, of having our identity shaped by what others think of us. God is out there and up there on the mountain, "Father God." And everyone knows that the people on top are entitled to more money and privileges, for there is a hierarchy of wealth, education, and position in the church. The rich, the educated, the bishops all deserve the best. Stage 3 churches and individuals are always busy. Sunday mornings are a hubbub of activity. Ministry is performance, most of it self-centered, and leaders are frequently burned out. The bureaucracy blossoms, and legalism may abound. People earn doctor's and master's degrees by passing courses and are given a union card to practice ministry or therapy or teaching. Trying to please others or keeping control takes precedence over listening.

Yet God and the culture beckon individuals and churches to grow. More and more education calls for the sharing of stories, feelings, and reactions. Business leaders know that a rigid top-down structure will not compete in the culture of permanent change, so a different kind of structure and leadership is necessary. And the pervasive quest for spirituality seems to infiltrate churches, businesses, and universities at many levels. It's hard to keep the living God at bay.

There is an in-between stage that we might think of as Stage 3.5. These people may seek meaning at a deeper level. They may be disillusioned with what the culture calls success. They may suffer, as the disciples did, the death of their ideals, the death of the God they used to believe in. People in adolescence and young adulthood may be here. They are interested in values and spirituality but not the religion of their parents. They have begun to notice their soul and to move away from group-imposed values. They vote independently. They don't go back to church because it's the thing to do. They "church-shop" and look around for spiritual teachers.

Stage 4. People at this stage often can listen because often they are letting go of the boxes in which they have put God, and the boxes in which their thinking has resided. They typically want something more. They often have stopped trying so hard and can begin to surrender to God more fully. They don't have to be in control. They can learn from others without shame. They like organizations of peers, and often "Manage By Walking Around" (a current corporate byword), just being there. Often they are the seekers who have surrendered their knowledge of God as inadequate. People who have been trained to think skeptically now become open to the limits of thinking and embrace mystery.

For people to deepen spiritually, they apparently need a spiritual support system. Small groups can operate quite well in business, teaching, church, and research. The groups may be formal or informal. Mature people need others to encourage them to take the next step individually as well as to move together. God is often spoken of as Holy Spirit, Christ within. Salvation is belonging, coming home. People listen to each other, hear the need for change, and listen to God on the inside. Ideally, people and groups at this stage are in touch with the Spirit and quite able to ask for what they need. The dark side may be that mature stage 4 people are more obsessed by their becoming or spiritual search or type of prayer than with the reality of God.

Spirituality training centers for spiritual directors need to warn against seeking again and again the experience of God more than the God of experience. I remember in my training, we were urged to ask, "Where is the call of God?" in any feeling or lack of feeling.

While every transition is difficult, the transition from stage 4 to stage 5 may be called "the dark night of the soul" or "the wall." It is a more difficult transition because a greater surrender is called for. Leaders have difficulty in relinquishing control and not taking it back. Janet Hagberg, a Minneapolis writer, says in her book on stages that ordained, intellectual, guilt- and shame-ridden, high-achieving, and doctrinaire people have a hard time at a spiritual wall. My experience is that one encounters many walls, many stuck places. Life and God invite us to move on.

Stage 5. This stage is fairly rare in the church or anywhere else. Often these are the people who have retired, who are tired of church work, and who want to follow a call within a call. Mother Teresa of India talked about her mission to the poorest of the poor in terms of a call within a call to be a nun. Others will serve those in emergency housing, take on Habitat for Humanity projects, or serve in a mission overseas. Individuals here may love paradox and mystery as ways of thinking about God. Some give up speculative thinking and do the thing God gives them that is at hand. They may continue to have a sense of the presence of God. They may study other traditions without falling into relativism. Self-directed learning is the norm: people write books or papers, travel on pilgrimage, go off on long retreats. Some of my friends say that they don't do anything that isn't fun, but by fun they mean fully engaging and meaningful. They tend to be more balanced with work and play to the point that it may be difficult to tell them apart.

Organizations at this stage are highly flexible and respond to the external and internal movements of the Spirit. The organizations live in the now. Some may train and contain mentors and guides. At times the teaching and support groups of which I am a member function at this level. We have an exciting interchange of ideas, and the work becomes like a dance or like a jazz improvisation. The basic patterns have been learned so that it's possible to do variations and innovations spontaneously. It feels at times as though the Spirit were working, thinking, singing through us. There is no hierarchy, and decisions are made by consensus.

Organizations and individuals at this stage are not without a downside, at least from the view of outsiders. Individuals may be out of touch with practical things. They may not care about denominational concerns or every form of social injustice. They may not seem to be productive. Groups may depend too much on consensus building, and become clumsy and slow. They may be too compassionate for victims and become gullible. They may throw out all tradition. They may focus so much on the process that they lose sight of a goal. Some say that only after we have arrived here can the real spiritual pilgrimage begin.

STAGES OF SIN

How is sin manifested at the various stages?

At stage 1, sin is simpler even than Adam and Eve. *Sin is self-protection*: everyone out for self. When we revert to this stage from fear or rage, we become a mob; we are less than animals, who usually kill only out of need for food. How is it that that a group of well-developed people can suddenly turn demonic and destructive? There is a mysterious quality of sin that rationality cannot deal with.

At stage 2, sin is more like the story of Adam and Eve, who violated the prohibitions of God. *Sin is experienced as rebellion.* All of us have stolen apples or reputations, crossed the boundaries of law, and lost our innocence, We can't go back again. A hierarchy of the strong seek to claim all the money, power, and sex.

The perversions of stage 3 may be the worst, because of a power differential endorsed by the community. *Sin may giving too much power to leaders*, failure to grow, not using the freedom God has given. Violence, abuse, boredom, and depression are the symptoms of the failure to be the ones God has called us to be. Women need to be themselves—find their voice. Men need to learn to reach out and ask. A healthy mutual dependency is needed to grow. In my view, a 12-step program like Alcoholics Anonymous or Sexual Addicts Anonymous is needed on an ongoing basis to help sexually or chemically addicted people to admit their lack of power, to acknowledge the necessity of asking God, to surrender, and to face regular confession and the making of amends. There is a far more robust sense of sin and grace in such programs than in most churches.

There is a danger that people going through stage 4 will identify stage 3 as the enemy. Most management consultants see stage 3 as the one to move beyond. I believe that stage 3 is a great accomplishment for human history and for an individual. In the 12 steps, it is a major step of liberation to believe that there is a higher power greater than our addiction or lack of freedom. We need God and others.

What can be sinful at every stage is our fear of those in the stage ahead, or our rejection of those in the stage we have left behind. Judgment begins with the house of the Lord, with us. First, we need to cast the bias from our own eye, and then we can see the sin in others. This is true of individuals, congregations, and denominations.

The perversions and sin of stages 4 and 5 are described well by C. S.

Lewis in *The Four Loves* and *The Great Divorce*. Lewis says that each of us has a besetting sin of which we need to let go. Lewis knew that all our loves need conversion, that even the highest loves require transformation by God. It is surrender all the way up, abandonment to divine Providence all the way along. Only it gets a bit easier to recognize the necessity to repent. Living the Christian life is like sailing a small boat. We can't control the wind, the gusts that come and go. We may tip over. But after this happens a few times, we don't waste time in the water but admit that we made a mistake, turn the boat upright, and try again. A monk, asked about the spiritual journey of a resident of the monastery, said, "We fall and we get up." I believe that continued self-examination in the presence of God and accountability in one's spiritual and professional life are necessary.

WHAT BUSINESS ARE YOU IN?

My friend Ed White, a senior consultant for the Alban Institute, often asks churches, "What business are you in?" A lot of churches are in the business of providing a wonderful worship service on Sunday. Others are in the business of providing a nice religious museum for a handful of the like-minded. Some are in the business of getting people involved in activity, particularly to work for justice in the world. White says that there is just one business that the Gospels describe: the disciple-making business. "Go and make disciples of all nations, baptizing them in the name of the Father, Son, and Holy Spirit, teaching them to observe all that I have commanded you, and lo, I am with you always, to the close of the age" (Matt. 28:19-20).

Disciple making includes evangelism, worship, and teaching. The early church had none of our fancy programs. It grew disciples by their life together, prayer, fellowship, and teaching. The images for stages that earlier people used were more rural and agricultural: first the blade, then the ear. Growing up into Christ. No longer children. Jesus had in mind that the disciples would grow through what I describe as the five stages—finally to become mature. He wants us filled with the Spirit, in the body of the church, reaching out, witnessing in the world.

Exercises

1. At what stage are you, right now? What do you think God may be asking of you as the next step? Is your experience illumined by stage theory?

2. Where is the leadership group of your congregation? What might God be inviting you to do and be?

3. Where is your congregation? Where might God be calling you to grow?[2]

CHAPTER 3

Love Differentiates

"Happy families are all alike; every unhappy family is unhappy in its own way." That's the way Leo Tolstoy's *Anna Karenina* begins. I didn't agree with that statement the first time I read it, and I disagree with it more and more. Tolstoy didn't know much about happy families; he died as an old man, running away from his wife. When I worked as a counselor, I noticed that people with addictions were remarkably similar. On the other hand, those who are creative, the geniuses, the self-actualizing, the saints, are quite different from one another.

Two great spiritual guides, Baron Friedrich von Hügel and his directee Evelyn Underhill, knew that souls were unique and different from the beginning of their spiritual journeys and became more so as they grew. While these two English spiritual writers wrote knowingly about mysticism and the spiritual life, they had a healthy regard for differences. One size does not fit all in spiritual growth. Even spiritual stage theory can be used simplistically. It may be comforting to think that all people in a particular stage are similar. Actually they are no more alike than all northerners or all Americans. We may start out assuming that we know which books will make sense to someone else, what kinds of prayers will suit another soul, how God is dealing with another. I certainly have made that mistake again and again. I hate to think how many sermons I have read that assume that the preacher's experience is normative. Yet the paradox is that the more unique and specific my story, the more often someone else will recognize a bit of his or her story in it. If we take into consideration the differences in learning, experience, and development, it is a wonder that we can communicate at all. Even when I look at my closest friends, those who have been educated the way I have been, who may score the same as I do on a personality test, I see that we are different. (Indeed, the radical differentness of our friends may be one definition of friendship, as C. S. Lewis suggests.) So how can we get outside the myopic view we all have? Perhaps most profoundly, we can do so by continued surrender to God, so that we are not so ego-centered. But until we arrive at that point, my experience is that maps, visual charts, the more the better, help me expand my understanding that others are different, and how they are different. Maps in the physical world describe the experience of a community greater than my own. I present here a map, a way of describing differences, for two reasons:

- Learning about other types of spirituality makes leaders more adept at speaking different languages.
- Learning my type can affirm my path and keep me from trying practices that don't fit me, that may be detrimental to my personality.

For years I used the Myers-Briggs Type Indicator as a way of teaching people differences. My former congregation used the type descriptions as a way of helping to match people with jobs. But teaching and learning the Myers-Briggs system is hard work. To do it right involves administering or taking a long test, scoring it, and then teaching or learning a new language of psychology.

Recently I found a shorter way of getting at differences, one that doesn't require psychology. It is based on the research of Urban Holmes, who was dean of the School of Theology at Sewanee, Tennessee. He noticed that historically, similar patterns in spirituality were repeated over the centuries. One distinction can be made between those who know God intellectually and those who know God in their feelings and intuition. Then there are those who use images and words in prayer versus those who find silence, mystery, and imageless spirituality most helpful.

Corinne Ware's book *Discovering Your Spiritual Type* is based on Holmes's work.[1] She has designed a short written test that can be taken in 10 minutes or so. Ware has a background in psychology and teaches at the Episcopal Seminary of the Southwest in Austin, Texas. When I first read the book, it seemed too simple. But I found others who used it with congregations and who found that it was an excellent way to begin talking about spirituality with people who weren't in the habit of talking about their experience.

Participants in a seminar can take the Ware sorter in 15 or 20 minutes, calculate the results, and then chart their type and their congregation's type in an hour. Participants then have some common language to talk about their experience and see how it is different from others' experience. They can also report how they see their congregation as a whole (usually quite limited) versus the variety of people in the congregation. Ware cautions against oversimplification, but the reason I rejoice in her test is that it is simple; there are no ladders of perfection, no character flaws mentioned, and so there is little chance of harm from misuse. I recommend to leaders who want to teach others that they buy and use her book. She digs into theory and details and offers a much more elegant testing system than the one I use here. I have relabeled her categories for the groups I work with, and she has graciously affirmed my choice of labels.

When I have led seminars with clergy groups, leadership teams, and Sunday school classes, people usually find great affirmation and relief, saying, "I'm so delighted that I don't have to force myself to pray that way." They can see that they are different from some people and similar to others and that the differences and similarities are not a problem. And people show great interest in scoring their congregation's type versus their own. I recently taught a class in the congregation whose pastorate I left several years ago. There were new members who had joined since I left, as well as old-timers. I found, for instance, that most of the older members of the congregation I had served were quite similar to me. Big surprise. And the new members who had joined after I left were very much like the new minister. There, on the chart of our types, was a graphic presentation of our preferences, one that we might talk about to help people understand the differences between the newcomers and the old-timers: no right, no wrong; only differences.

What can the pastor and other leaders do when they discover that while the congregation represents a wide variety of people, Sunday morning seems to focus on one type only, the type of the current pastor? I think that this distinction is a natural phenomenon but one to work against. Were I to go back to my previous congregation, I would be even more insistent on involving people from all four points of view in the Ware instrument to help plan worship, and I would ask representatives from these four, and from different generations to give me some in-depth feedback about where God touched them in the service. I wouldn't limit the evaluation to the group present, of course, but would use some objective criteria from the history of liturgy and the gospel.

Figure 11
The Four Types of Spirituality

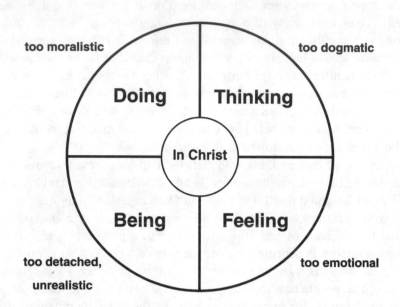

I have renamed the four spirituality types "Thinking," "Feeling," "Being," and "Doing." The originator of the types arranged them in a circle, thereby suggesting a circle of wholeness, that all four belong in the church and in individuals if there is to be a balanced spirituality. Each type has its excess, which tends to be heretical and isolating. As all four move toward the middle, toward each other, toward the mystery of God at the center of our individual and corporate lives, they become more whole. There may be a natural movement toward the opposite quadrant.

Here is a quick sorter given to me by Corinne Ware that you may use to select your type. Take it for yourself first, and then for your congregation as a whole.

USING THE SELECTOR

In figure 12 (page 48) are two numbered circles. One represents the congregation's spirituality, the other yours. The 12 numbered sets of statements represent spiritual themes. In each set, number 1 describes the intellectual or thinking type; 2, the heart or feeling group; 3, the mystic or "being" type; and 4, the visionary action or "doing" segment.

Read all the statements. You may find several with which you agree, or none. Put a slash in the appropriate quadrant of the "Myself" circle for each statement that applies. Then, after reading the statements again, mark the quadrant of the "My Church" circle that seems to fit your congregation's spirituality.

After all have finished, the leader can transfer each participant's "Myself" slashes to a large flip chart, and similarly add each person's mark to the "My Church" circle. Use a heavier line for the pastor's slash. Then reflect on the results. Why do most of the slashes show up in the quadrant with the pastor's mark? Put the individual scores up, and reflect on the implications for the congregation.

People generally start in one quadrant; at times such as midlife they may switch to the quadrant diagonally opposite, providing more balance.

1. Thinking Spirituality

This group of people favors sermons, lectures, and study. My guess is that the majority of professors in seminaries are in this group. Content is important, and a coherent way of thinking about God and things of the spirit is important. Prayer is verbal, often written. A common danger is overintellectualization, with one's ideas about God replacing the reality of God. Another danger is that because this group winds up predominating in seminary, pastors may assume that adult learning is the same as undergraduate study, and that more ideas and techniques are what people need in order to be leaders. The growing edge for them is to learn to enjoy God, to be with God without having to talk or be productive. They need to study theologians who wrote before the Enlightenment to see the proper place of reason as a part of experience.

Listening and Knowing for This Style. People in this quadrant may be attracted to the knowledge about God that becomes knowledge from God (the shift that many thinkers describe from rationality to worship, receptivity, and listening). C. S. Lewis said that when he was studying theology, prayer came naturally. Other thinking people say that they know the Truth as they consider truth, as Calvin did when he talked about objective truth

Figure 12
Spiritual Style Sorter

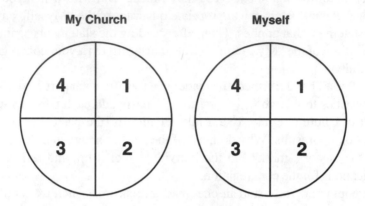

The Order of Worship
1. A carefully planned and orderly worship program is a glory to God.
2. A deeply moving and spontaneous meeting is a glory to God.
3. Simplicity and some silence are important elements needed for worship.
4. It is not a service, but ordering ourselves to God's service that is important.

Time
1. Stick to announced beginning and ending times of worship services.
2. It is important to extend the meeting time if one feels led to do so.
3. All time is God's time. A sense of timelessness is important.
4. Gather whenever and for as long as you need to accomplish the task.

Prayer
1. Words express poetic praise; we ask for knowledge and guidance.
2. Let words and feelings evoke God's presence in this moment.
3. Empty the mind of distractions and simply be in the presence of the holy.
4. My life and my work are my prayer.

Music
1. Music and text express praise to God and belief about God.
2. Singing warms and unites us and expresses the soul's deepest heart.
3. Chant and tone bring the soul to quietness and union with God.
4. Songs can mobilize and inspire to greater effort and dedication.

Preaching
1. The word of God, rightly proclaimed, is the centerpiece of worship.
2. The gospel, movingly preached, is the power of God to change lives.
3. Proclamation is heard when the Spirit of God speaks to the inward heart.
4. What we do is our "preaching" and speaks louder than anything we say.

Emphasis
1. A central purpose is that we fulfill our vocation (calling) in the world.
2. A central purpose is that we learn to walk in holiness with the Lord.
3. A central purpose is that we be one with the creator.
4. A central purpose is that we obey God's will completely.

Support of Causes
(If necessary, circle the words that apply and note categories with the most circles.)
1. Support seminaries, publishing houses, scholarship, preaching to others.
2. Support evangelism, missions, spreading the word on television and radio.
3. Support places of retreat, spiritual direction, liturgical reform.
4. Support political action to establish justice in society and its institutions.

Criticism
1. Sometimes I/we are said to be too intellectual, dogmatic, and "dry."
2. Sometimes I/we are said to be too emotional, dogmatic, anti-intellectual.
3. Sometimes I/we are said to be escaping from the world and are not being realistic.
4. Sometimes I/we are said to have tunnel vision and to be too moralistic.

Dominating Themes
(If necessary, circle the words that apply and note categories with the most circles.)
1. Discernment, discipline, knowledge, order, grace, justification.
2. Love, conversion, witness, spontaneity, sanctification.
3. Poverty, humility, wisdom, letting go, transcendence.
4. Simplicity, purity of heart, action, temperance, obedience, martyrdom.

Member Criteria
What the congregation believes is necessary, who you believe is necessary.
1. Assent to doctrine; baptism; endorsement by group.
2. A personal inward experience of God, baptism; public declaration.
3. All who face Godward are incorporated in the holy.
4. Solidarity with humankind is membership in God's kingdom.

Ritual and Liturgy
1. Ritual and liturgy evoke memory and presence, teaching traditional truths.
2. Liturgy and ritual ceremonies are not of great importance.
3. Ritual and liturgy are ways in which God becomes present to us.
4. Ritual and liturgy are one way we make statements about inner conviction.

Concept of God
1. God is revealed in Scripture, sacrament, and in Jesus Christ and his cross.
2. I can feel that God is real and that Christ lives in my heart.
3. God is mystery and can be grasped for, but not completely known.
4. We participate in the mystery of God when we become creators with God in the world.

Used with permission of Corinne Ware.

Figure 13
Spiritual Type Growth

	1	2	3	4
Start	intellect-theology vocation spoken content	affect, heart-warmed tears personal renewal stories delighting	searching being keeping inner silence meditating	action=prayer focused assertive
Deepen	solitude (look at 3) introspection keeping silence interior experience feeling	social justice (look at 4) thinking acceptance of other styles broad vision	inclusive (look at 1) (look at 2 & 4 especially) critical reflection teach others	God has control (2) lightening up enjoying God now
Escape	head trips rationalism loss of feeling dogmatism, dryness	too exclusive "my walk with Jesus is better than yours" caught in feelings	too exclusive self-absorbed self-protective passive	moralism tunnel vision intellectualism
God	mystery	love	I AM	kingdom
Prayer is	wonder thoughtful contemplation	heartwarming storiees intimate presence	silence	action
Meditation	interior listening privacy	listening to others listening to God	including others	enjoying

Figure 14
Worksheet for Spiritual Type Growth

Which number (from the chart "Discover Your Spiritual Type") describes you most of the time?

Begin with START. Can you remember a time when God seemed real, when you seemed most alive, centered, connected? Make a few notes.

What abour DEEPEN? Are there times when you are stretched past your comfort zone?

Look at ESCAPE. If you identy with items on the chart, do these attitudes tend to remove you from God, life, others, connectlons?

Do you agree with the practices listed under PRAYER IS? If not, what is prayerful? What connects you wlth others and your spirituality? Are there activities you like to do that you might call prayerful?

How might you do more?

Think about MEDITATION or "listening." How do you listen to yourself, to God, to others?

How might you correct the chart?

How might you be more intentionally prayerful?

and the inner testimony of the Holy Spirit. People with this style may switch to quadrant 3 and use some sort of contemplative prayer. They become aware of the limits of logical thinking and appreciate the mystery of God that cannot be understood or controlled. John Macquarrie, a theologian, was obviously in this position. In an article called "Prayer as Thinking," he wrote: "Those Christian activists who make much of mission but little or nothing about prayer are rarely themselves good representatives of the Christian mission."[2] He went on to say, "What they need is contemplative prayer, prayer which is silent before the face of Christ. This may involve thinking: 'To pray is to think in such a way that we dwell with reality and faith's name for reality is God.'"[3]

2. Feeling Spirituality

These people want to know God with their feelings. Mainline congregations, along with charismatic and postmodern groups, are moving in this direction. This heartfelt spirituality may not always be demonstrated in dramatic displays of emotion alone, but may be found in religion that appeals to tradition, sentiment, meaning other than rational. For those in this quadrant, the presence of God is felt. There is a movement of the heart. People here may tell stories of God in their lives, often with great ease, and frequently want others to experience the same delight and joy in God as they have.

One of this group's weaknesses is wanting everyone's heart to be "strangely warmed" like theirs. They may also identify the presence of God with some emotional state, and then think God has abandoned them when this feeling passes, as it will. Their growing edge is to obey, to do, to find God's will in doing the ordinary.

Listening. I think that listening prayer for people in this quadrant comes to focus on the reality of Christ, rather than on subjective feelings. Christ is there in worship, scripture, others—in every word that comes from God. Listening prayer may be learned by asking, "Where is the call of God in that situation?" I find that the best way to ask myself the question is by using the daily *examen* that Ignatius of Loyola teaches. Ignatius, the late Medieval synthesizer of spiritual exercises, considered the daily examination supremely important. In modern garb, this *examen* offers a way of looking for God in daily events within and outside the self. But instead of focusing just on God's gifts or my sin, the focus has become where I sensed God's presence, or God's absence, during the day. In the case of God's gifts, gratitude is the response. In God's absence, I ask for help. Some days I don't remember to pray a listening prayer because I'm too distracted by many things, but I am finding that I can be open to God while I'm writing and listening to others.

3. Being Spirituality

Corinne Ware calls this the "Mystic quadrant," but I prefer the term *Being*. Every quadrant can be mystical or contemplative, in my experience. *Being* seems to describe the relative absence of thinking or feeling or doing. The people in this quadrant easily find God in just being with God, or "hanging out." They may talk about listening to God, or wondering at God's creation or delighting in another person. There may not be any feeling or ideas here, only the mysterious "Be still and know that I am God" (Ps. 46:10). Many people in this quadrant who grew up in traditional churches leave the church to find God in nature or Quaker silence or Buddhist meditation. Many schools of spiritual direction are in this quadrant. They call themselves contemplative and often believe themselves to be more advanced than thinking- or feeling-centered people. These people often want to stay in a state of contemplation all the time and may find it hard to relate to ordinary people. Their growing edge may be using their intelligence to appreciate how God may use other people. They may also move into being more ordinary and less "special," to being contemplatives in action.

Listening. Often people in this quadrant may focus on techniques. That's often destructive, in my experience, for I see spiritual direction clients who are "centering" (a popular style of meditation) twice a day and have no sense of God when they are not centering. The point is not my state of awareness but my noticing God. One is a focus on me or my technique; the other is a focus on God. A recent biography of Julian of Norwich, a Medieval English mystic, says that by the end of her life, "she has broken with the elitism of the contemplative. . . . In the last analysis, the important thing is faith, not feeling."[4]

4. "Doing" Spirituality

Corinne Ware calls this "kingdom spirituality," or "crusading spirituality," and it is the quadrant where people do things for the kingdom of God. They have a passion for transforming society, for social justice, or for individual acts of compassion. Frequently these people say that they have no time for quiet prayer, but practice the presence of God as they are working—"contemplation in action." Ware says it is the smallest group, certainly in most churches. I think of the "Doing" quadrant as made up of people who are not compulsive about their activity, but do it just for the joy of doing. They may be artists or truck drivers or youth workers. When I ask some of my friends where they find God, they say it is when they help, serve, and do. Perhaps their growing edge is to learn to be in touch with their feelings. Others I find who say that they are in this group are those active in efforts to bring social justice, and they don't seem to burn out. They evidently find energy in doing. Their chief weakness may be superficiality and lack of development.

Listening. My experience is that these people do not go to classes in spirituality, and many do not go to church. They may be attracted to walking a labyrinth or walking meditation. But most often they are the ones rebuilding houses for Habitat for Humanity, helping the homeless, running the stewardship drive. Some men like men's movements and parachurch organizations like Cursillo. The French spiritual writer Jean-Pierre de Caussade wrote, "To be satisfied with the present moment is to relish and adore the divine will moving through all that we have to do and suffer as events crowd in upon us."[5] He continues, "We may take up some special kind of devotion, a particular pious practice. . . . God will step in and upset our plans."[6]

Jesus calls us to listen; these people listen in action.

CONTEMPLATION

The word *contemplative* is confusing. Some think that the word describes only those in the "Being" quadrant and then try to get all the other quadrants to be like that. This kind of thinking demands that we all be still, practice centering prayer, and not talk about knowledge of God. I think that the words *contemplative* and *mystic* are not the property of any one group or style of prayer. I try to use the word to mean paying attention to God.

Spiritual writer Kathleen Norris tells us that "The writers of the early church used the word 'contemplative' to convey their experience of the presence of God."[7] Another writer, David Steindl-Rast, says, "To contemplate means raising our eyes to a higher order that challenges us to measure up."[8]

Everyone can have, and probably has had, a direct (contemplative, mystical) experience of God. Many of the meditation centers that nurture spiritual growth and train spiritual directors often assume that a few kinds of silence, listening, or contemplation are the paths to growth for everyone. This assumption may work well for a Roman Catholic religious order, or for a small cross-section of a congregation, but it won't if your purpose is to minister to a whole congregation. My experience is that the third quadrant's definition of contemplative prayer can suit the spiritual needs of perhaps 10 percent of a congregation at most. Spiritual directors who try to minister to a whole congregation usually fail unless they realize that they are encouraging a spiritual elite. People in all of the quadrants need to recognize that the best kind of spirituality is the kind we do best. One hopes that we begin to learn *our* style of contemplation by using the material provided here.

PRACTICAL OBSERVATIONS

I find that using the material about spiritual types in a group is much preferable to reading it by myself. It's relatively easy to catch on to the ideas, but in a rather superficial way. In a group you can immediately see the differences in people's types, and recognize that your point of view is limited. When I help a church board to describe its corporate identity and members' individual identity, people make all sorts of connections. I usually give people a chance to find their own type, and then to report how good the fit is. I ask about worship, going over the statements in the sorter, and have people discuss their common worship. This exercise usually results in a telling "Aha" about some of the church's internal wars over worship and music.

What about your congregation's style of worship? The church I attend has three services; each has a different character. The first service has no music, and provides long pauses for silence. It seems perfect for the "Being" people in quadrant 3. The second service serves families and uses a contemporary liturgy; informal, heartfelt music is sung—a perfect service for "Feeling" people (quadrant 2). At 11:00, a more formal liturgy is offered, and more people wear dressy clothes. I suspect that the "Thinking" style predominates there. I once preached at all three services. My jokes got laughs at the first two services, and were met by stony silence at the third. My guess is that services aimed at unchurched "seekers" are usually designed for "Feeling" types.

I find that teaching about spiritual types in a group helps everyone deal with individual patterns and helps promote group understanding. Just seeing friends and fellow parishioners who are different from oneself stretches the mind. At times I have invited people to wear nametags with the label of their quadrant, or to move to designated corners of the room.

In a spiritual growth group or in dealing with an individual, knowing the chart may give one a guide to listening. If someone uses the thinking style and reports that she is tired of books and is beginning to be attracted to silence, it may be easier to affirm that this shift is the Spirit working. If someone else is a feeling, heart-centered person and his wonderful warm feelings about God's presence vanish, an understanding of spiritual type may help him to understand that God may be weaning him. Then he might look for more ordinary ways of being present to God and others. If the other is a "Being" person and prayer has stopped being the way she likes it, she might be invited to consider that God is calling her to try a different style of prayer. If the other is a "Doing" person, he will probably want a feeling kind of prayer. I find that God continues to call me past my favorite type of prayer. The point is first to affirm the natural starting place; second, to notice when God calls us to grow to include another style; and third, to focus on the ways God comes to us. Most people need to be affirmed in their natural pathway in the beginning of their journey. Farther along, many people give up on God and prayer when they don't get what they like: healing, warm feelings, a sense of direction. At this point spiritual growth requires surrendering more deeply to God, finding God in hidden places that are often in plain view.

Exercises

1. Try taking the sorter, which is a very brief way of finding your type.

2. Score "My Church" and "Myself."

3. Where are the similarities, the differences?

4. What type is the pastor?

5. What do you learn about trying to minister to all four types in worship? About teaching spiritual formation?

CHAPTER 4

Where Do We Start?

About 10 years ago, psychiatrist and author Gerald May came to town to talk to a group of spiritual seekers. He had just published a fine book on prayer, *Addiction and Grace*, and was well known for his other books and his leadership at Shalem Institute for Spiritual Formation in Washington, D.C. I was there and I saw colleagues who were spiritual directors, teachers, clergy, and dedicated laypeople.

At one point in the conference May invited questions. One listener rose and said something like this: "Dr. May, I'd like to know what to do next. I do centering prayer for 20 minutes, twice a day. I read the Bible contemplatively. Through the day I practice the presence of God. What's next?"

May paused, smiled slightly, and said to the questioner, "I don't know. Why don't you ask Jesus?"

At first I thought the reply was just too clever. But his words sank in. Many of us are like the questioner, trying to do our spirituality thing. At times it sounds as if we are collecting pious techniques, trying to prove ourselves to God or to ourselves, focusing on our spiritual practice. Sometimes I think we are spiritual overachievers. May was right: ask, pay attention to God. We're in a relationship, not a competition.

ASK JESUS

So how do we ask Jesus? In Matthew Jesus says to pay attention to what God is doing, to God's gifts.

> What I'm doing here is to get you to relax, to not be so preoccupied with getting, so you can respond to God's giving. . . . Give your entire attention to what God is doing right now [Matt. 6:31, TM].

God is giver, gift and giving, continually communicating with us in many ways. But until we pay attention, we don't receive. For most of us in church, this journey begins at birth or at our baptism. Our conscious awareness may happen in church. We may start our conscious awareness of a spiritual journey with an experience of transcendence, of joy or wonder or love or affection or feeling at home. So start with your experience, the spiritual story of when God was real for you. For those who haven't grown up in a religious tradition, I may talk about the experience of belonging or wonder or longing. Then I describe four areas:

Creation

Is there wonder at mystery? Is there indignation at pollution? Have you ever felt delight in an animal? Have you wanted to go beyond the beauty to the source of all beauty? The questions by themselves may not help people remember. With some groups poetry may strike a chord; another group may relate to movies. Most groups respond to stories that others tell.

Structures, Groups

Has singing or worship or music ever made you feel connected? Has this experience been joy or sorrow? What happened inside you? Have you ever felt patriotic or in despair for our country? Has the Vietnam Memorial or the story of Auschwitz or Corregidor stirred you? Have you felt a part of a team in sports or at work? Again, a movie may stir us, presenting truth or beauty. Or life itself may. I remember a meeting in college at which a member of the East Harlem Protestant Parish spoke about injustice in New York. I felt a call to ministry.

One-on-One

Have you ever felt affection for your surroundings, ever had a friend, ever been in love, ever received love? The mystery we call God has the name of love, belonging. Ask the mother and father of a retarded child to talk about their courage in loving. Get out old pictures of your parents, your honeymoon. Look at the people in your life as a wonderful gift.

Inside

Have you ever felt at home in the universe, or in despair? Have you ever anguished at the suffering of another, or longed to be free? Have you ever felt guilt or shame? Have you ever been grateful? Many people are out of touch with their feelings. Men may look down on "touchy-feely stuff." Some have been taught to be ashamed of their tears, to deny all feelings of anger. It may be easier to start with positive feelings and then read some of the psalms, unedited by liturgical experts. Whenever I read the Palm Sunday story and yell, "Crucify him!" or utter "How long, O Lord," I am empowered to express my feelings to God.

Some wouldn't think of their experiences as being religious or spiritual unless they are noticed and shared and confirmed by others. I think we do a disservice to God and others if we begin our evangelism conversations by quoting scripture or trying to raise someone's awareness of sin. Why not listen to how God is acting in the other person's life? There will be time for talking about sin and scripture in God's own time.

REMEMBERING

I frequently open a retreat or seminar by asking people to remember a time when they felt at home, or experienced joy or longing or wonder or truth. Then I ask people to share one-on-one, and we collect our experiences in a group. We begin to notice our inner "facts," the inspiration of the Holy Spirit. On our own, we often pass right over what is happening, but skilled spiritual formation helps us notice what we feel as a fact of experience. We learn to share this feeling with God. When our experience is affirmed by others, we learn a hallmark that we then can use to measure other experiences. This affirmation is similar to joining a Presbyterian church a hundred years ago. New members were asked to share their spiritual experiences, and were then affirmed by the group. Most people today have only their *ideas* confirmed as worthy of respect, so that they forget or demean their own experience. Religious experience isn't just our subjectivity, for our experience can be confirmed by others and by scripture. When individuals come for spiritual direction, I spend an hour or two listening to their story and reflecting on what I notice in their religious experience.

Another way to begin the spiritual journey is to notice where prayer is going on right now. The Apostle Paul wrote: "We do not know how to pray as we ought, but the Spirit intercedes for us with sighs too deep for words" (Rom. 8:26).

Peterson translates this passage: "If we don't know how or what to pray, it doesn't matter. [The Spirit] does our praying in and for us, making prayer out of our wordless sighs, our aching groans" (Rom. 8:26 TM).

The theologian Paul Tillich said: "Words, created by and used in our conscious life, are not the essence of prayer. The essence of prayer is the act of God who is working in us and raises our whole being to himself."[1]

God is at work in our longing, our sighing, our praising that may hover below the level of awareness. Our heart and body know better how to connect with God than our mind and superficial feelings do. If I feel my prayer is too abstract, I get on my knees. I delight in coming to communion for the same reason. Jesus doesn't say, "Understand this in remembrance of me." Often Jesus is in our lives as he was with the disciples in the storm on the Sea of Galilee, asleep in the boat while they were concentrating on the storm. We may be able to notice him in our busyness and attention to the externals of life. Many traditions in the church teach a daily act of noticing, called inventory or examination. The point is to pay attention to what God is doing on a daily basis. Beginning at such a place differs markedly from beginning with a book on types of prayer. For years, I started praying as though it were my project, my doing, without considering that God was more interested in my prayers than I was, that God was like the father of the Prodigal Son running down the road to receive his boy home. God is more interested in our church and small group and marriage and life than we are. But we're like one of the two sons—one getting his speech ready, the other focusing on his duty resentfully. When we start with paying attention to God, it is like seeing all parts of the story of the Prodigal Son, which really ought to be called the story of the Prodigal Father.

Jesus teaches about prayer in the Bible. He gives us a name for God: "Our Father." But "Father" isn't quite the right word. The Aramaic word is "Abba," which means "Daddy." Traditional Jewish prayers often exalted God's holiness; Jesus, on the other hand, stresses the intimacy of our relationship. Paul says that only the Holy Spirit can bring us to a place of this intimacy; it is not our achievement. "When we cry, 'Abba! Daddy!' it is the Spirit himself bearing witness with our spirit" (Rom. 8:15, 16 TM). But we can ask for this gift. So secondly, after suggesting that people begin where they are, I encourage them to ask for what they want. It may initially be healing or peace, but as the relationship continues, we may ask for love, for

God's presence, for God's will. Jesus also says, *"Our* Father." It is not God and I alone. I am praying for the community; the community is praying for me. Some traditions also include feminine names for God.

Jesus teaches us to pray that God's will be done. Many people pray this prayer again and again without asking what it means specifically. I remember the character Elwood P. Dowd in the play and movie *Harvey*. When people said something nice but meaningless, like "We ought to get together sometime," he would ask, "What did you have in mind?" To ask God "What did you have in mind?" is to get specific about God's desire, God's hope, to align myself with God's will by becoming willing. I often teach a visual way of alignment. I read the story of blind Bartimaeus and Jesus (Mark 10:46-52). Bartimaeus cried out for help, and Jesus said, "What do you want me to do for you?" Or "What did you have in mind?" I ask people to put themselves in the place of blind Bartimaeus. We are all blind when it comes to noticing God. I ask people to imagine Jesus saying, "So what do you want?" What is your passion? I give them time to tell Jesus what they have in mind. Then I ask them to ask Jesus, "What do you want? What is your passion for me?" and imagine Jesus' reply. What does Jesus have in mind for me? Frequently people can imagine Jesus' reply. They share with each other to confirm or ask questions about what they heard. With practice it gets easier to discover God's will for the moment.

FIND YOUR PRACTICE

When a person has told God what he or she wants, has listened for God's passion, and has shared this discovery with others, a spiritual practice may be discussed. Instead of starting with someone else's idea of a spiritual discipline or practice, why not ask Jesus? Then the practice comes from God and not from our idea of being holy. For instance, if you really want to do God's will, and God's will is that you receive more of the fullness of God's grace, what kind of practice might you adopt that will help you receive? Walking outside, listening to music, reading a psalm? If Jesus says he wants to love you, forgive you, use you in ministry, how will you be able to listen continually to his guidance?

An awareness of God's initiative is critical. Some churches give out long laundry lists of what to do as spiritual practices. Many books offer long descriptions of spiritual disciplines. Attending to specific directions can lead to guilt, resentment, or excessive worry over whether we are doing it right. Why not ask Jesus? De Caussade wrote: "We may take up some special kind of devotion, a particular pious practice. God will step in and upset our plans."[2] He continued, "There is only one rule for us: the duty of the present moment. The soul is as light as a feather, as fluid as water, simple as a child and as lively as a ball in responding to the impulses of grace."[3]

I believe that religious practice should serve our relationship with God. If you want a relationship of love with God, a spiritual marriage, then spiritual disciplines are necessary to grow. But instead of reading books about disciplines, ask God. Pay attention.

Start with Jesus' words, by addressing this God as "Daddy," "You," "How great Thou art," or whatever name comes from your heart. The name may surprise you, as it must have surprised the Medieval English mystic Julian of Norwich, who prayed, "Jesus our Mother." Start noticing where God speaks to you most often: scripture, nature, relationships. One of my favorite quotations is from Samuel Miller, former Harvard University chaplain:

> Let your soul speak for itself. Some souls hold conversation with God in music, and some in the sowing of seed, and others in the smell of sawed wood, and still others in the affectionate understanding of their friends. Quit dressing yourself in someone else's piety. Untie your soul, give it room to breathe, let it play, do not be ashamed of it. It is the child of the eternal and destined for greater things than you dream."[4]

Try a Group

Many people do better at finding their practice in a group where their experiences are affirmed. My material "Stop, Look, and Listen," described in appendix B, is designed to help people pay attention to God in groups and alone. Many people are afraid to use their imagination to hear God speaking. What if we make a mistake? All through the Bible people used their feelings and intuition to say, "Thus says the Lord." If we are in a community that can sort out what we hear, if we are continually in touch with the Scripture and what it reveals as the character of God, then if we are wrong, we can easily be corrected. We're talking about an ongoing relationship, not a final examination.

What comes bubbling up as you pray? Frequently people come to mind whom we should visit, or apologize to. Sometimes I write a dialogue with Jesus, recording his words as well as mine. These words from Jesus aren't just my own fabrication, for I am often surprised by them. They ring true: they sound like the voice of the Good Shepherd. Sometimes I get a sense of what is right, or an awareness of where I am off base. As I check with my body (you're tired, working too hard) or my relationship with my wife (When was the last time we went out together?), or my relationship with God. (Quit worrying about doing this right; I love you; receive my love), I frequently get a nudge that can be put into words.

But I do best in a group in which people are talking about their relationship with God, relating what they have heard. Some churches have an unwritten policy about spiritual practices: "Don't ask, don't tell." Exchanging experiences of the spiritual journey seems more private than speaking of sexual experience. But keeping ourselves so well defended ensures that we will not develop a vocabulary for our spiritual experience, won't learn from others, won't enjoy the validation that comes from telling our story and eliciting a response. The community doesn't receive the gift we have to share. I usually appreciate the rough stories of beginners and the stumbling stories that leave a lot to the imagination. Best of all is a group where we tell individually what God is doing in our work and as we meet. Frequently the Spirit is working similarly on all three levels.

Clergy

As Anglican theologian Martin Thornton observed, "While individuals may go deeper, the overall climate of the congregation will not go further than the clergy and core lay leadership."[5]

The spiritual vitality of clergy is a priority in any congregation. And yet most clergy I have seen are so busy with ministry that they cannot or will not put first things first. Clergy have a special problem. They handle holy things and ideas so much that they think knowing about God is the same as knowing God. Or they get bored and say the right things without the words being hooked up to their minds or hearts. As a consequence, for most of the clergy I have worked with—evangelical or liberal—prayer and personal spirituality have atrophied. Clergy are adept at praying for any occasion and can read the Bible with an eye to preaching a sermon. But usually they have no one to share their spiritual journey with, no group, no spiritual guide. They are usually not accountable to anyone for the most important part of their ministry. No wonder they are burned out or leave the ministry.

Finding a spiritual director has been a great breakthrough for most of the pastors I've taught. The Spiritual Exercises of Ignatius of Loyola are very compatible for most Protestants. Ignatius teaches people to pray with scripture; and his stages of growth, the four weeks, are quite familiar. One Jesuit said that the stages are similar to the kinds of love C. S. Lewis describes in *The Four Loves*. Spiritual directors can be found in most medium-size cities. Spiritual Directors International (see appendix E) can give references. I think that there is wisdom in finding someone in a different denomination than one's own. It may be helpful for a young man to find an older man for mentoring and direction. The most important credential I look for is someone who is in supervision and who has a director for his or her own work.

Some clergy start finding support by discussing sermon ideas or what is wrong with their parishes. I found this helpful at first, but it is nothing like having a trained person listen to me alone for an hour, to have some silence for me to reflect on what I have noticed, and to answer evocative questions. Mature people who have had some direction may get to a point at which simply sharing with a good friend is enough. I have found that clergy can benefit from a group of three for listening to each other (see appendix D, handout 7). Clergy and other professionals often want to "fix" each other, but once the group has met for five or six sessions, the structure begins to work and the participants learn to listen to each other and to God.

Another help for pastors is a group for case studies (see appendix D, handout 6). Some disciplines are necessary for the group to get past bragging or complaining. When I organize such a group, I follow some variation of a classic pattern. Prayer surrounds the exercise. Someone presents and answers factual questions and then is silent. The others prayerfully consider the situation and talk about the dynamics of what has happened, including where God might be working in the situation and in the presenter. The presenter responds. Clergy need to be able to ask for help and to discern where God is in their parish and within themselves. After a while the group may become more informal, after the participants have internalized the questions about God's presence. I am appalled that more clergy don't practice peer supervision. Even if not in a formal group, clergy ought to have access to some kind of peer meeting to receive feedback. Virtually every trained psychotherapist is in some form of supervision, and so is any good spiritual director. This continual learning is far more helpful than a weekend seminar or the latest gimmick that promises instant learning. Change and growth take place over time.

Professional Growth

Businesses and churches have recently begun training coaches to promote professional growth. Much of the coaching consists of helping a person develop a mission statement and areas to grow in, and supporting the professional's process of moving in that direction. I have moved toward that approach in my spiritual direction of professionals. I find that despite traditional spiritual direction that focuses almost exclusively on our inner life, our meeting with God is not only within, but in relationships and in our ministry. We are not created to be alone but to be connected in community.

I believe that anyone who has a responsibility for the spiritual guidance of others should be in a relationship of accountability with another for the sake of the people he or she guides, teaches, or preaches to. Otherwise we are going to grow, if we grow at all, in a deformed shape that will be passed down to others. I see such distortions frequently. It is a biblical concept to be accountable to someone else. Timothy was mentored by Paul, Paul by the disciples in Antioch. Friedrich von Hügel, author and spiritual director, once wrote: "Behind every saint stands another saint. That is the great tradition. I never learnt anything myself by my old nose."[6]

So for church members I recommend this as a starting place:

1. *Stop, look, and listen.* Watch and pray. Pay attention to God's absence or presence, God's gifts and calls. Try writing down what you pray, what you notice in life, scripture, or your heart.
2. *Find a small community.* Get a friend or two colleagues, and start by helping each other pay attention to what God is doing now. Perhaps a program that gives you some starting exercises will be helpful.
3. *Address God personally,* ask for what you want, and listen for the answer. It may not be the answer you want, but there will be an answer. It may be hidden to you, and you will probably need friends to help you listen for it.

See the bibliography for books that might be used by small groups. For clergy in particular, I recommend:

1. Reread 1 Timothy, particularly Eugene Peterson's paraphrased version, from *The Message*. Paul says: "The first thing I want you to do is pray" (1 Tim. 2:1 TM). "Exercise daily in God—no spiritual flabbiness" (1 Tim. 4:7, TM). Some sort of spiritual exercise is a necessity for the sake of those who serve, as well as yourself. Learn to read scripture as a vehicle for God to speak to you, not as a text to teach or preach from. I have known professionals who cannot use the Bible this way, but who must quiet their minds in some form of meditation free of image or idea. Pay attention every day to what God is saying in your body, your relationships, your church, and your awareness, from scripture. There will be times of simultaneity when all the channels seem to be used by God.

2. Find someone to talk with about your soul, for your sake and for the sake of the people you minister to. The same person may be able to reflect about your ministry as well, or it may be better to do this reflection with a group of peers.

3. Find a group of leaders or potential leaders to mentor. You will probably learn as you teach and as you listen. Go through a book that guides you together into sharing and discerning the Spirit. But do more than read books. Ask those whom you mentor what they notice when they pray. Ask where God is calling. Ask where they encounter "the mystery that we call God."

4. Read some good theology from your church tradition. Spirituality is not a modern fad but the passion of God's people for ages. More important, speak about the passion of God. Stand in awe of God's grace, grandeur, and glory.

5. Read some history. Read about people in a different century, a different tradition. My experience is that I see things when I'm away from home that help me come home with new eyes.

6. Avoid successful authors who claim to have the answers; avoid big rallies filled with signs and wonders. You may benefit from a group designed for clergy by the Alban Institute, where meditation and theology and practice come together. Pay attention to the ordinary in your life and your parish. I remember telling my spiritual director that "nothing is happening" in my prayers. She said, "Tell me about that nothing," and in a relatively short period of time I came to recognize the Holy Spirit in subtle ways in me and in my parish.

Naturally I know all these approaches because I have made many mistakes. You may not have to make all the classic mistakes but rather hurry on to your specific character flaws and blindness.

Boards

I address the church governing board as a whole, believing that board members' function is to be spiritual leaders. Boards stand at different places. Some are driven by getting the work done in much the same way that any other organization does. Here are some suggestions of how to start.

If the board is at stage 2, the leader must take the initiative, read scripture and the rules of the denomination that give guidance for leadership. The pastor may have to seek allies to start expanding the opening prayer into a Bible study that includes a time of sharing about what we think God wants us to do. With my leadership group I proposed a check-in time along with tighter control of the agenda so that we finished at the same time. A meaningful shift is to move from having a debate on issues to having a dialogue. The leader might use a management book like Peter Senge's *The Fifth Discipline* as a tool to persuade businesspeople in stage 3 that corporations use this material. At least, ask for silence for a while and ask people to speak their truth without debating what someone else has said. If this device doesn't work, ask the person who speaks to repeat what the previous speaker has said, to the satisfaction of the previous speaker. This procedure is very close to the active listening model taught in many disciplines. If there is no consensus, ask people to pray about and discuss the issue for a month or two.

The board retreat can be an excellent time to introduce individual and corporate models of discernment—one task of spiritual leaders. I usually alternate an exercise for individuals with one for the group as a whole. I start with remembering where God has been in the past for individuals and the congregation. Then we listen to scripture individually and corporately. We ask Jesus to speak and tell us what he desires. The retreat should be a time for people to relax, share individually, get a sense of the Spirit's movement in us individually and as a group. My preference is not to do a lot of small business, but to get the big picture and to renew the vision and call for both the board and for individuals.

Boards can set the style for the committee structures of the church, and a corporate spiritual style can move from committee to community with check-in and discernment. Boards can understand that the training of spiritual leaders happens as they meet, as they check in with their personal stories and try to discern where God is leading them corporately. The training of new officers is a great entry place, where people can tell their stories about God and learn to do both individual and corporate discernment.

Congregations

For congregations, the starting place depends on the state of the parish. When I'm called to be a consultant on congregational spirituality, I usually use the charts in chapters 2 and 3 as a beginning. I tell people that these charts are like stories and ask them to put themselves in a part of the story. When participants place themselves on the developmental stages, they have begun to diagnose where they are in the story of the disciples. Then we consider the question "Where might God be calling you?" If a church is at stage 2, some boundaries and rules are most likely necessary. There needs to be a higher power, a sense of the law that Moses handed down, some structures that define who has what power. Try reading sections of Psalm 119 that rejoice in the law. Stage 3 churches may hear a call to an inner spirituality. Businesspeople may know about "leading from the inside out." Someone may want some silence or sharing as in a 12-step meeting. When I am delightfully surprised by a stage 4 going to stage 5, I am usually amazed by the creativity that bubbles up. I find it's helpful to use the Corinne Ware material (see chapter 3). Congregations are often surprised to learn what their corporate style is, and usually find that they are not speaking to all the circle, all the types. Growing churches usually have lots of leaders in the second segment in Ware's schema, that of feeling. People in all of the quadrants see why they have a natural affinity to some and not to others. Perhaps small groups or adult-education offerings might be labeled or advertised more accurately, according to type. (This might include a seminar for thinkers who want to discuss issues, a caring-and-sharing group for intimacy, silent prayer for those who feel called just to be with the Lord, an action-planning seminar for social justice.) Later, the groups that plan worship and education may be able to be more deliberately inclusive. My lectures and sermons are slanted differently for groups that have different styles of learning and prayer. Another helpful approach is Quaker author Richard Foster's book *Streams of Living Water*. This is a simply written history of spirituality, showing five streams (contemplative, holiness, charismatic, social justice, and evangelical). No matter what tradition a group is in, it helps to learn about others and to wonder what this other tradition can teach us about growing in grace.

I try to listen for a congregation's corporate angel. Recall in the Book of Revelation the Spirit's speaking to the angel of every church. People in the ancient world believed that an angel ruled over every structure—as a benevolent force or a destructive one. We might talk about corporate culture, or the spirit or soul of a congregation. I usually talk about corporate culture and give parishioners feedback about what I have heard as they have worshiped and shared stories. In short, I deal with a congregation as I deal with an individual: I ask, "Where is God, what is your fondest prayer, what is going on?" The questions may help people know a corporate entity that is more than a sum of all the individuals, a "we" that individuals can become aware of.

For most churches the easiest place to begin to listen to God is in worship. Leaders may provide periods of silence for people to do their own praying, silence for people to listen to scripture without being told what it means. After the service parishioners can reflect on what helps worship and what hinders, where they encountered God and where they were bored. I consistently hear parishioners in liturgical churches wanting to know, "Why do we have written prayer, which is so boring?" I see others looking at their watches. "Why it is all done for us? Where do all these writings come from?" Several Episcopal priests of my acquaintance preside at an "instructed liturgy"—the sermon time for three Sundays is spent telling people why they worship as they do. These priests' experience in teaching this instructed liturgy has been that everyone, newcomers and old-timers alike, appreciates worship more. It is like understanding the structure of the Bible or the spiritual dimensions of an icon.

In my experience, a poor way to begin spiritual formation in a congregation is with a spirituality committee. I formed such a committee in one congregation, and the outcome was a fight for turf in adult forums and in designing programs for everyone else. A spirituality formation committee also tends to attract members who are more than beginners, and they may push their own favorite practices—like the labyrinth, centering prayer, or *lectio divina*. These practices may appeal only to a select group of members. Ordinary people may feel that if these practices are examples of spirituality, they don't want any part of it. With wise leadership, spiritual formation may be seen as a cooperative venture for the whole congregation. Knowing what I know now, if I were to organize a spiritual formation committee, I would include representatives from the worship committee, the governing board, adult education, children's work, and stewardship, and prayerfully consider what could be done throughout the congregation. The senior pastor and other clergy would need to be actively involved. And so would the members of the whole congregation.

From my own experience, I found that another ineffectual way to begin is for the pastor to talk about spirituality all the time. In a church I once served, people used to beg me to find another topic. I love to talk about my primary passion, but I would have done far better to listen to members' experience of God and to speak to that. Preaching needs to start with listening for God in the congregation. This listening is probably what pastors of an earlier era did on their pastoral calls. Richard Baxter, a Puritan divine, had all his parishioners call on him once a year, and asked each about the state of his or her soul. Were they at peace with their neighbors? Did they know some of the Creed, at least that God loved them? Did they pray regularly? When I left the last parish I served, an older parishioner said that no pastor had ever asked her how her soul was until I came. How can leaders listen to parishioners in a language they can understand?

WHERE IS GOD CALLING?

I think that paying attention in every area—worship, board, adult education, mission groups, youth and children's ministries—might mean to continue asking the question "Where is God calling?" What does Jesus mean in saying, "Go out into all the world"? Do we exist for the sake of others? What does it mean to make disciples? Do the stages of growth the disciples experienced constitute a model for our church? What are we to teach? Only ideas? Is learning the same as growing? Are learning from our life and listening to God almost one and the same? At some stage, it may be helpful to lead a program of spiritual formation with the whole congregation. The last time I helped my former congregation with a congregationwide program of spirituality, we conceived of it as asking questions for five weeks. These questions were addressed to individuals and the congregation as a whole.

1. What are you grateful for? What gifts has God given us? What has God been doing?
2. What do we want? What matters to us? What do we deeply desire?
3. Is it really God I hear? How do I discern God's call? What is in God's heart?
4. What can we do to hear God better? What kind of practice do I need in order to listen?
5. How can we help each other? How can I get support? How can I live faithfully?

People told stories each week as part of worship The preacher preached on the theme for the week. We gave everyone a booklet with daily exercises on the theme and arranged a feedback class for people to share their answers. In appendix B, see a fuller report of this process, titled "Stop, Look, and Listen."

Another way to involve the whole congregation is to work on a mission statement together. The process of writing the statement can be quite brief. In the parish I served, leaders were asked to draw simple pictures illlustrating where they had seen God at work in our midst. I was greatly surprised that no one drew the community at worship. This outcome opened my eyes because my point of view was the pastor's. One effective way to involve the parish is to invite individuals to read passages in the Bible for two weeks and to make notes. After studying these same passages in sermons and groups, then the congregation can reflect in small groups: "Where has God been active in our life? Where do you think God is calling us?" These responses can be put in priority order on the basis of scripture and the wisdom of the group; then they may be printed and distributed to the congregation for prayer and reflection. Then the board can respond to what the congregation says, offering suggestions for programs or process. Material about writing a mission statement is found in appendix A.

Another way to start is inspired by the book *Natural Church Development*, by Christian Schwarz, head of the Institute for Natural Church Development, located in Germany. He describes a whole system of material to help congregations.[7] His approach begins where the church-growth model ends. Schwarz decided to find out what was really happening in churches that were growing. He questioned leaders and members of 1,000 churches around the world. He found that no one gimmick dependably worked—such as "seeker services" or other packaged formulas that proved

effective for some churches. Instead, the author found eight qualities, natural ones. When these were working at a maximal level, growth took place.[8]
These eight characteristics seem rather obvious:

1. Empowering leadership
2. Gift-oriented ministry
3. Passionate spirituality
4. Functional structures
5. Inspiring worship services
6. Holistic small groups
7. Need-oriented evangelism
8. Loving relationships

Schwarz's approach is complementary to the one I offer here. As far
as I can tell, he engages in more diagnosis of strengths and weaknesses
than discernment of God's call, but he is interested in strucrure and spirituality and gives a hint of where to start. His approach by itself is not designed
to help people and churches listen to God. To me, it seems tone-deaf to
social justice. But if individuals and the congregation are reading the Bible
and newspapers, and living together and listening to God, the channels are
likely to be open for God to call for justice.

CHANGE

If a congregation starts listening to God, change will take place. I was in a
group that used to talk about its spiritual pilgrimage in terms of the people of
Israel leaving Egypt. One person might report that she was still in Egypt
spiritually. Another might say he was in the desert and dry. Another would
comment that she was at an oasis. Never did any of the group report being
in the Promised Land. This omission was probably not due to excessive
humility but rather to the realization that when the people of Israel reached
the Promised Land, they still hadn't "arrived." God was always calling them
to something new. And so are we called, and the change has been speeding
up.[9] According to current management theory, only flexible organizations
will survive. No longer will top-down attempts to manage suffice. Small,
flexible groups are being given as much responsibility as possible in growing
corporations.

What does the rapid change in the culture do to the desire for stability in congregations? I like the old hymns I've been singing all my life. They, like churches and icons, become more hallowed with age. We remember the meaning from the past and are nurtured spiritually. I am shocked when my young friends tell me that they can't stand "my" music. It is a challenge to incorporate new parishioners who say that they can't worship in a museum. And the newcomers differ among themselves. Some love gospel hymns; others prefer Lutheran chorales. Some like popular Roman Catholic songs, while others like praise choruses. Even wilder is worship at "new paradigm" churches that project the words of the songs on a screen. Often I can't detect a pattern in words or music that I'm used to.

Managing change is an art and something that can't be done by the numbers. Yet I believe that the stage theory we've been using has something to contribute. Stage 2 churches need order—most likely external. They need to have boundaries and the rule of law before they can enjoy true freedom. To introduce new ideas in this sort of church, the pastor needs the support of the matriarchs and patriarchs who really run the parish. Stage 3 churches need deliverance from too much outer order so that the inner vision, the corporate character, the witness of the Holy Spirit, may lead. The senior pastor's approval and leadership are necessary here. Stage 4 churches need to move from the doubt and uncertainty they usually feel to inner clarity and then to outer service and ministry.

When the whole leadership group can pray and listen to God, when the congregation can be involved from the start, change happens. Jesus provided order and spiritual formation for the disciples as young men in stage 2. He used the authority he had to send them out as stage 3 people. He helped to prepare them for knowing him in a new, internal way. As they waited in the upper room, a stage 4 experience, they prayed, waiting for the power of the Holy Spirit to send them out with new power. One way of managing change will not work for all churches.[10] Here are further details:

Figure 15
Change in Congregations

Stages	2	3	4
Power	Held by patriarchs and matriarchs— small handful	Exercised by clergy and board	Ideas, initiatives bubble up from the community as the church shares the Holy Spirit's gifts
Source of Authority	Expertise or status or tenure	Control by reason, law, vote	Comes directly from God, revealed in scripture creeds, life by the Holy Spirit
Nature of Change	Change happens very slowly, when threatened or afraid of chaos	Change happens when those in power say it should and then top-down	Change happens quickly. High level of trust, delegation, often consensus

Congregations at stage 1 or 2 can be quite dysfunctional and need a strong leader to give power to the church board rather than to the resident patriarch or matriarch.

Young or new clergy are likely to have problems with change. Frequently the new clergy change the order of service to reflect the latest theory or book studied in seminary. The service may employ more or less inclusive language, encourage hugs or do away with them, specify that worshipers kneel or stand to receive the communion elements. Some churches just don't care about these details and are used to change whenever a new pastor comes. Other congregations will stand for gradual changes that are convincingly explained. Still others have argued fiercely over the liturgy or other issues. To change the practice even slightly opens up a can of worms. New clergy are often admonished not to change elements of the worship service until they figure out the unstated rules. The admonition is not always helpful, however. One parish I served was so eager for change that I was told not to consult but just to go ahead. Another parish needed an elaborate consultation with many people to understand the varied wishes for new and old hymns. Another parish's pastoral leadership seemed to be open to varied input, but the final decision was made by the senior pastor, and he was often swayed by one or two parishioners.

Some parishes in stage 2 don't want to work on a mission statement. They may be in a working-class neighborhood, where people are used to old-style management, with the bosses "envisioning," and the workers carrying out orders. A consultant friend works in a working-class suburb and finds that no one in the parish wants to come up with a vision. Two miles farther out, a suburb filled with executives has lots of members who want to be part of the "visioning process" but not many people who want to work at carrying out the vision. Folklore has it that most clergy have grown up in large suburban churches and have little experience with members who expect someone else to do the planning. That is why I recommend for stage 2 churches that the clergy find a small group of leaders and do the "visioning process" with them. Obviously, the process should be shared with the congregation.

In short, a new leader in a congregation ought to have an idea of the congregation's current stage, and begin where people are—but gradually work toward the next stage if possible. It is a mistake to treat a stage 2 congregation as if it were at stage 4. This error is frequently made by young pastors fresh out of seminary. The matriarchs and patriarchs won't let change happen and will informally or formally sabotage the plans. The new people unto whom much freedom has been given will easily become discouraged. For if change is to take place, a transition through stage 3 is essential. Rules are needed—rules that can override the wishes of the old network of leaders. At times the new pastor in a stage 2 church must talk with the patriarchs and matriarchs—but then announce the denominational rules for decision-making. A good interim minister will do the same.

Stage 3 churches are likely to make a big production out of studying the need for change, and then come up with a big plan. The problem: this new plan will probably be out of date in two years or so. The goal for stage 3 congregations is to decentralize decision-making, and most stage 3 congregations find change threatening. In my experience, it is often the older men, the bankers and accountants and small-business owners who resist delegation of authority. The younger entrepreneurs, women, and people in research and development or technology will most likely be experiencing decentralization in their professions and will probably already be functioning this way in the church.

Where do we begin? What's next? Why not ask Jesus? I've made suggestions about listening. Could it be that some expert doesn't have the specific answer? That Jesus has something to teach you uniquely?

Where do I start? Listen to what Jesus says. Where do we start? Notice what Jesus is doing in our life together. Not "What would Jesus do?" but "What is Jesus doing?"

Exercises

1. What do you as an individual do to listen to God's call? Where is God calling? What kind of support will you have?

2. As a leadership group, where is God calling you to grow?

3. As a congregation, where is God calling you? How do you discern this call together?

CHAPTER 5

Discernment

As individuals and congregations begin a practice of listening to God, decisions must be made. What kind of spiritual practice shall I begin? How do we listen to God when we make decisions on a governing board? The answer: by discernment.

Discernment is not a special spiritual word. In common usage, it means to distinguish one thing from another. A discerning choice is one made by a person with the ability to chose well. The discernment question for Christians is: "Is it God we hear and follow?" Discernment comes after we have listened to God. Discernment is inviting the mind of Christ to decide on a basis other than ego-centered choice. The process of church discernment is wonderfully described in Acts 15, which concludes, "It seemed good to the Holy Spirit and to us." Debate, silence, prophecy, and witnessing each played a part. The process of discernment is that of distinguishing the Holy Spirit from other spirits:

> Don't believe everything you hear. Carefully weigh and examine what people tell you. Not everyone who talks about God comes from God. There are lots of lying preachers loose in the world. The person who has nothing to do with God will, of course, not listen to us. This is another way for telling the Spirit of Truth from the spirit of deception [1 John 4:1, 6 TM].

Different spirits inhabit our world. We have the responsibility for telling one from the other. One principle for discernment is correspondence to the revelation of God in Jesus Christ—there is a similarity between what God is doing now and what God did then. Another in scripture is doing the will of God, not just saying, "Lord, Lord."

We usually want to discern the best course of action when we have a big decision to make. We want to know God's will. Shall I go to seminary? What's the mission of our congregation? In the long run, the goal is not only to make a right choice now, but also to know the Lord whom we serve, to live a life of listening and responding, to live in community with God. So discernment usually starts as a process with a decision to be made, and can become a style of life. Practically, discernment by a church board is usually saved for important policy issues. Discernment on a personal basis may be asking God daily for direction, guidance, and help.

I have always liked "Open My Eyes," a 19th-century hymn of discernment. Clara H. Scott (1841-1897) wrote both the text and the bouncy tune:

> Open my eyes, that I may see
> Glimpses of truth thou hast for me;
> Place in my hands the wonderful key
> That shall unclasp and set me free.
> Silently now I wait for thee,
> Ready, my God, thy will to see;
> Open my eyes, illumine me, Spirit divine!

Discernment processes are all a commentary on Jesus' teaching us to pray, "Thy Kingdom come, Thy will be done." There are many decisions we don't need to discern, but we may need guidance to apply them. The Ten Commandments and the tradition are quite clear as to God's will on some subjects, both for us to do and to refrain from doing. But some directions are not clear. Some choices, evidently, God gives to us to decide because it doesn't matter to God what kinds of flowers we plant in front of the church. Other decisions—such as our call in life, what our church should do now—seem important to God and to ourselves. Evidently God wants us to have free will, to grow in our ability to make good decisions, to mature. Here is what I understand to be the wisdom of the church on discernment.

1. *Discernment is telling the voice of God from the other voices we hear.* What voices do we hear that are not God's? A colleague teaching a class on discernment asked participants to pay attention to what was going on in their heads. There were critical voices, questioning voices, voices speaking that caused guilt or shame, and so forth. Then she asked the group members to imagine that they were listening to Jesus. What would he say? They wrote down their imaginary words of Jesus and shared them aloud.

The writings were remarkably consistent. Jesus said he loved them, affirmed them, and told them to relax and let his love in. To the class, it was clear that God spoke in a voice different from that of the ego and destructive forces.

2. *Discernment is a way of knowing.* In the Old Testament, to know (*yada*) is personal, bodily, nonintellectual. Adam knew his wife. People are urged to know the Lord, which is not intellectual knowing. John Calvin, reformer and theologian, said:

> The Christian philosophy, though
> Would have reason yield, retire,
> Give place to the Holy Spirit,
> Subject itself to His direction,
> So that man no longer live
> To himself alone, but have within himself
> The living, reigning Christ.[1]

The Spirit brings us the reigning Christ. We know the sound of his voice.

3. *Discernment is an art and a gift.* Discernment is an art that improves with practice. We get a feel for God and we know how temptation sounds. We say, "Oh, you again!" to both sin and God. We are able to share our discernment with others, and they can confirm some insights and ask questions about others. This is partially a human skill that improves with practice. Part of the practice is sharing with others, both for individual and congregational listening. We develop a vocabulary to describe the inner witness of the Holy Spirit. We need the feedback from others.

Discernment is a gift from God. God is not an object to be studied. God is the subject who speaks, decides, reveals what God wants to. God gives us an open ear, a heart that can be touched, a capacious mind. Discernment is the art of receiving these gifts.

4. *Discernment is different for different styles of people.* Obviously French-speakers hear God speaking French. God is heard differently by all of us. Discernment is learning to use our language. The language of discernment differs for different styles of people. For "thinkers," God is usually known best in the word. ("The word is very near you; it is in your mouth and you hear." [Deut. 30:14].) For "feelers," God is usually revealed first in heart knowledge, in the language of relationships or music. ("Believe in your heart" [Rom. 10:9].) For those whose style is "being," God may be

known first in the stillness. ("And the Spirit speaks with sighs too deep for words" [Rom. 8:26].) And for those whose spiritual path is primarily "doing," God may first be revealed in action, with reflection coming only afterward. (Jesus taught the disciples on the way to Emmaus, and afterward they reflected.)

My experience is that we start listening to God with our favorite language; then life and the Lord teach us more. Group discernment seems to work better when all the spiritual languages a community knows are practiced. We need each other's gifts to make good decisions, to know the Lord's presence. I go out of my way to select people of different types or gifts to give me feedback about a worship service, to give me feedback about articles and books. I need to hear from outsiders and from people of different generations.

5. *We don't learn discernment from a book or a sermon.* We learn discernment by doing, by paying attention to our experience of God and having it confirmed by others. Most of us know God in retrospect. In Exodus 33, Moses says he wants to see God's face. God puts him in a cave in a rock, and passes by, and says that Moses will see the backside of God. We understand that we usually can't know the fullness of God face to face, and that it is only afterward that we can notice where we have sensed God.

6. *We know God in our experience, as we gain some practice in listening.* We can grow in awareness of God's voice, God's presence, God's guidance. We can talk about stages in awareness, steps on life's way. Before modern stage theory Søren Kierkegaard wrote about stages along life's way that people might pass through. Ignatius of Loyola said that the stages of his spiritual exercises needed to be practiced in a particular sequence, and that there were different rules for discernment for the first and second stages of growth. Almost all who write about prayer and discernment say there is a difference between discernment for beginners and discernment for those more practiced. I offer a simple chart, a way of thinking about the stages and practices of discernment. Like most charts, it is oversimplified. But it does offer a guide for leaders in a congregation who want to start a process of discernment with individuals and their congregation. As the chart indicates, some practices are easier for beginners.

Figure 16
Stages in Discerning

	1	2	3
Individual discernment	Join a church. Worship. Study. Tell your story, your uniqueness, gifts.	Be able to tell the Direction you are oreinted—toward God or away; willing or willful. Can hear God's call.	Moment by moment, dwelling in the light. Aliveness. Awake to God in all people.
Practices	Devotional Bible study. Daily awareness. Keeping a journal. Writing your mission statement.	Daily examination of consciousness. Small-group accountability.	Detached ego. Accountable to someone for spiritual and professional practices.
Corporate discernment	Worship that helps participants notice God in scripture and life. Small groups that ask, "What does God say? What will you do?"	Board and congregations can listen to God's call yearly. Decisions are made worshipfully.	Interdependence in leadership.
Practices	Write a mission study. Discover corporate spirit. Celebrate faith-sharing.	Mission statement used to evaluate programs. Congregations and mission recipients give continual feedback.	Several methods of corporate discernment. All levels listen to God.

Ernest Larkin has written one of the simplest, yet most profound books on discernment I've read. Larkin is a Carmelite, a member of the order that specializes in the spirituality of Theresa of Avila. He uses the stages that Ignatius synthesized from the experience of the church to that date. Larkin's book *Silent Presence: Discernment as Process and Problem* suggests three stages of discernment. His writing is about individuals. (I have added the material about congregations.)[2]

STAGE 1: APPLICATION OF SPIRITUAL DOCTRINE

We start the life of discipleship by learning the truth, however that comes to us in our tradition. For me, this means starting with the Bible and with C. S. Lewis's *Mere Christianity*, with standard Christian belief and practice. I take Lewis's definition of "mere Christianity" to be close to the center of the tradition. Here, in this step, we may study the history of the church, scripture, and theology, to get a general sense of God's character. God loves us. We are invited to love God and others. This is the first step of spiritual formation.

I took this step in seminary. I wanted to know what the truth was, what was orthodox—that is, what was believed by most Christians most of the time. I wanted to know what was in the Bible and the God who revealed himself therein.

For those in 12-step groups, the first steps are admitting powerlessness and asking for help. (The "doctrine" is often stated thus: "Stop drinking and go to meetings.") This "doctrine" is very much like the four spiritual laws that many evangelicals use. (We are created good, we fall, Christ died for us, and we can surrender to his grace.) We learn that we are powerless and need a higher power.

We learn how to speak the truth. We begin to trust the community. We learn how to listen to the stories of others. Essayist Kathleen Norris said that when she re-entered the church, she was put off by the language. "Doctrinal language slammed many a door in my face and I became frustrated when I couldn't glimpse the Word behind the words. Ironically, it was the language about Jesus Christ, meant to be most inviting, that made me feel most left out."[3] If there's anything worth calling theology, it is listening to people's stories—listening to them and cherishing them.

It is important to tell our stories of belief and unbelief, where we have longed for something more, and where we have been found. It is also important to have our gifts affirmed. We gain some self-knowledge about our gifts and our character flaws. Being acknowledged is the foundation for all future growth.

We learn to ask, "So what's the truth?" when feelings overwhelm us. We learn to trust in God rather than in our thoughts or feelings. Many people in the Eastern Orthodox tradition repeat a small piece of scripture again and again when they go through temptation or great pain. I hear "Come unto me." Jesus is the Truth. He is the sacred Word to whom the words of doctrine point.

Many people find it useful to write a personal mission statement to remind themselves of the objective call that they believe, no matter what their feelings are. Stephen R. Covey's *The Seven Habits of Highly Effective People*[4] says that we need to start defining ourselves from the inside out, to start with the clearest principles we know that are greater than ourselves that we base our lives upon. I started doing this years ago after a workshop sponsored by World Vision, the international evangelism and relief agency. I put God first, family second, and ministry third. Again and again my work replaces God and family, and God comes in a poor third. When I can write down what I think my priorities are and, better yet, what I think God's priorities are for my life, my fatigue or fear isn't as likely to direct my actions. When I have an ongoing support group with which to share my mission statement, it is even harder to escape. The group tends to remember my vision and my previous attempts to forget.

How do the young people of generation X go about applying spiritual doctrine? They usually don't believe that truth is objective, and they may be bored with scripture. This disdain for truth is a huge problem for postmodern people who find no objective reality in science, morals, community, or themselves. Usually I don't start with them by directly teaching doctrine. I try to learn if they find some hint of God beyond their feelings that come and go. They are usually touched by stories. I have found that movies also work as an objective portrayal of truth. In the last parish I served, I would use films as illustrations for sermons, and describe where I saw God. All of our newcomers were either very late members of the boomer generation or part of generation X—people in their 20s and 30s. We'd go to a movie together and then have a discussion. I'd invite people to join me to talk about the film, and to tell where they thought that God was in the work. This approach was their equivalent of doctrine: where the community finds the truth together. Usually there was a tie-in with scripture. Then we could talk about thoughts and feelings, and where the Spirit might be moving inside us. Discerning in community lessened the individualism and subjectivity. Several generations could agree that God was present. A pastor could talk about the stories of the Bible that said similar things.

I also invited new members (most of them young) to tell the stories of their lives in new-member classes. How could they identify the movement of God in their longing, in their being found, in their being touched by music? Some touch the mystery in art, drama, or literature. They can, with some coaching, find parallels in scripture. In new-member classes, people can share their experience. They may thus start with their own truth and then go to the truth of scripture. When we received members, the members of our board would tell their stories throughout the membership classes. We learned differences and similarities in the way that God acts. Where there is honesty in community, we can help each other as we tell our stories. We were blessed with recovering alcoholics who told honest, gritty stories; the trust and openness continued. This is my understanding of the application of sacred doctrine in community. This understanding was provoked by Kathleen Norris, who writes:

> At their best, the creeds are simple storytelling. They relate the history of salvation, as understood by Christians. . . . The Bible, [Demetrius] Dunn reminds us, is a world "where story carries more weight than mere doctrine and where a creed begins, 'My Father was a homeless Aramean.'"[5]

For individuals, starting places for telling their story and beginning to discern God are reading scripture devotionally and making a simple inventory of the day. Study of the stories of heroes and heroines of the faith is often fascinating. Writing a simple mission statement is often helpful. Exercises about spiritual gifts are important.

For congregations, it's important to reread and study what God has to say about the church. A simple mission statement can come from a brief study. It is usually helpful to delve into denominational history, to have the point of view of other generations. One may find pleasant surprises about the passion and spirituality that existed then.

STAGE 2: RECOGNIZING FEELINGS

This second stage of discernment calls for recognizing feelings and deciding what to do with them. By "feelings" the Jesuits and John Calvin usually meant the things going on inside us that were not the product of our reason: insights, intuitions, emotion, movements that might be toward God or away from God. Spiritual directors often find that prayer is dead when people fail to notice and express their inner life to God, just as it is in other relationships. Noted early American preacher and spiritual leader Jonathan Edwards made a distinction between religious affections, which are deep and lasting, and feelings that come and go. If Edwards were a modern spiritual director, he would try to get at our deep orientation toward God, and have us ask that our heart might seek God. Trying to describe feelings is difficult when we use only our intellect. Feelings need to be expressed and shared in community, at least in safe small groups. Then we have a common language and can discern which of our thoughts and feelings lead us to God and which ones lead us astray.

Jesuits call this stage recognizing the various pulls on us: consolations and desolations. Consolations are whatever helps us love God more. Desolations are whatever pulls us in the opposite direction.

Tad Dunne, a Jesuit, rendered the *Spiritual Exercises of Ignatius Loyola* in a contemporary translation in 1991. He writes about consolation:

> At its peak it is an experience of love for God so direct that everything on earth, including intimate friends and relatives, is loved and appreciated as gifts from God. . . . It is not the same as feeling happy; it can include feeling grief over genuine tragedy. . . . It is an experience of feeling centered, at peace within, full of confidence in God. . . . It is any inner experience or state that enables us to make balanced judgments about reality and wise assessments about the value of persons, words, and deeds. . . .[6]

> Spiritual desolation is at its core the experience of loving neither God nor neighbor, but rather acting out of fear or compulsion.[7]

Learning the difference is a matter of each person's paying attention to his or her unique, inner experiences and realizing which ones to trust and which ones not to. We learn to stand back from sexual desire and say quickly: "So what's this about?" We notice that our anger quickly rises when we feel threatened, and we learn to see where this anger is taking us. Can we speak our truth and stay in community and in touch with God? Is this anger then helpful? Or is it cutting us off?

It's useful to know some of Ignatius' rules or guidelines that came from experience. When we are in desolation, we should make no decisions. We can't see the light when we're in interior darkness; we can't see God when our eyes are filled with tears. These times may happen because of outward crises like loss, pain, overwork, and stress. The desolation may be caused by abuse, addiction, work done in therapy, a change of identity (I'm retired now—who am I?). When we are in desolation, the rule is to ask for help. If you're depressed, go to a psychiatrist; if you feel rejected by God, tell God and ask for relief. We learn to thank God for consolation, for the gifts, for the direction of our life.

For the second stage, good questions ask about the direction toward which people are oriented. Handout 3 in appendix D may help. The question is a simple one: "What direction are you headed? Are your feelings, thoughts, actions leading you toward God or away?"

At stage 2, we also have to make decisions after we are in touch with our inner life. We need to make a commitment to follow God no matter what our feelings are. We are able to ask for help from the community. "Can you do what is right?" Mark Twain, the 19th century American humorist, once wrote to some schoolchildren with this advice: "Do the right thing. This will gratify some and surprise the rest."

Emotionally, we are able to detach a bit from our feelings and thoughts and can ask, "What is the truth?" Eventually we see that the truth is not abstract thought, nor our feelings, but incarnate in Jesus. We are able to devise some practice to listen to God in life and scripture and obey what we hear. "What is the call of God in this situation?" One spiritual director asked me that regularly. I was in the habit of analyzing an experience or decision to pieces. The question cut right to the chase, and I usually knew God's will intuitively. We usually know more than we think we know, and a good question may help us surrender our ego-centered knowing to the gift of the Holy Spirit. ("He will teach you all things and bring to your remembrance all that I have said to you.")

For individuals, discernment may begin with the detachment from surface feelings to ask, "What is the call of God here?" Individuals can also notice when they are in a state of desolation, cut off from God. They may ask whether they have been faithful to their relationship, or whether God may be using this period to wean them from having to feel good to know God. What happens to charismatics when their hands come down, to evangelicals who no longer feel the joy of the Lord, to mainliners who are no longer clear about the truth? This point may begin a period of darkness; the answer is not to try harder or give up but to surrender at a deeper level. God is trying to teach us in both our consolation and desolation to let go of disordered affections.

When congregations are in desolation, part of the answer for them may be to ask for help in discernment from the outside. Members may not be engaged in a church conflict but rather sunk in malaise, boredom, and apathy. Securing a spiritual director who can listen to the congregation as a whole may be appropriate here. It's usually helpful for individuals in this state to find a guide to help. Clergy can often benefit from talking to other clergy, and most people can begin listening to God in scripture and experience. A group can begin to practice dialogue and can write a more substantive mission statement.

STAGE 3: INTERPRETING FEELINGS

Interpreting feelings means a direct experience of God. Here we are able to ask, "So what is God saying in all this?" At this stage, it may be a normal experience for God to speak in our feelings and thoughts. To have confidence that we are hearing God by interpreting feelings, it is usually necessary to have passed through the purgation of stage 2. Purgation is an old word meaning that we are purified by noticing and detaching from our feelings and getting help. We start building our life on the truth. We are able to let God's chastening word speak to us about addictions; we are able to trust in God in all the storms of life. We have support from others in the community to help us keep on listening. Stage 3 is illumination—meaning that we know the truth. This truth is not only a statement of faith, but "I know that my Redeemer liveth." Now we can read scripture and find it speaking to us directly and simply. We are usually clear about where God is calling us and are mostly nondefensive in listening to those who are different from us, who challenge us and disagree with us. We are often willing to admit that we may be wrong about our politics and theology.

"Bill W.," the founder of Alcoholics Anonymous, wrote about the guidance possible in interpreting our feelings: "Here we ask God for inspiration, an intuitive thought or a decision. We relax and take it easy. We don't struggle. We are often surprised how the right answers come after we have tried this for a while."[8]

Bill W. describes the results born of experience: "Our whole attitude and outlook upon life will change . . . we will intuitively know how to handle situations which used to baffle us. We will suddenly realize that God is doing for us what we could not do for ourselves."[9]

This is living discernment as we listen to the Spirit in our souls. There are other phrases for interpreting feelings. Some call this "hearing a word from the Lord." Others say it is a nudge from the Spirit. It may be experienced as a leading, a conviction.

We can live at this stage as a community. We will cherish differences yet experience unity. There are times when we just know and don't have to talk a lot. Thomas Aquinas, the 13th century religious philosopher, said that this light "elevates our minds so that we can perceive things that understanding cannot naturally perceive."

We have a rich background of historic and scriptural truth, and we have a history built on God's truth, tested in the fire of experience. Now we can know God directly as friend to friend, lover and beloved, Abba and child. We know and experience communion with God. ("Abide in me, and I in you.") Calvin talked about his experience of union with God in communion that shocks many Calvinists who have only heard about Calvin's ideas. Martin Luther wrote about the Holy Spirit in ways that are hardly ever mentioned in Lutheran seminaries. He wrote to Peter, his barber, some practical instructions on prayer: "When such rich, good thoughts come, the other petitions should be omitted to give place to them, and we should listen in silence and by no means interrupt them. For it is then that the Holy Spirit himself preaches."[10]

We read or pray, and the word is in our heart. We hear music, and it penetrates our souls. We have the gifts mentioned in Galatians 5:22: affection for others, exuberance about life, serenity. "We develop a willingness to stick with things, a sense of compassion in the heart, and a conviction that a basic holiness permeates things and people. We find ourselves involved in loyal commitments, not needing to force our way in life, able to marshal and direct our energies wisely" (Gal. 5:22 TM).

Here we move past obvious right and wrong and go to inner motivation, attitudes of heart and mind, the riches of the Spirit. As Paul writes to the Corinthians: "We didn't learn this by reading books or going to school; we learned it from God, who taught us person-to-person through Jesus" (2 Cor. 2:6-7 TM).

At this stage it is useless to ask, "What word is from God and what word is mine?" or to talk about an "I-Thou relationship," because both God's spirit and our spirit act together. Jesus said we would be one with him and the Father. It is the mystery of communion, that Jesus abides in us and we in him. There is usually spiritual joy, both in good times and in bad times. the Spirit knows the spirit within us. It is the experienced spiritual director, the experienced spiritual group that has experience of the Spirit in life, that may give confirmation or questions. The movements of feelings or the Spirit within are affirmed.

For the third stage, there are more subtle criteria for discernment. Ignatius says the difference between the good spirit and the bad spirit is that the good spirit's leading is like that of water hitting a sponge: it is gentle. The bad spirit is like water hitting a stone: There is a jarring presence of my will versus God's.

A great master of discernment in American history, 18th-century New England cleric Jonathan Edwards, ministered in the midst of great revivals, where many lives were changed and a great deal of false or pseudo-spirituality was evident at the time. As Edwards listened and read his Bible, he developed a list of reliable and unreliable signs of grace. The unreliable signs were everywhere, and might or might not be the work of the Holy Spirit. The reliable signs, taken as a whole, were good indications that they were the fruits of the Spirit.[11] I've paraphrased some of them as follows:

Unreliable Signs of Grace

1. Intense affection or passion. We feel excited, close to God; things work out; we are touched. (This affection or passion may be perverted by our ego.)
2. The appearance of love, kindness, politeness. We have nice meetings where everyone agrees. (This, too, will pass.)
3. Feelings of assurance that we are saved, that we are being guided, that we are filled by God. (Hitler and lots of clergy were sincere in thinking the Führer was sent by God.)
4. Praise for God. (Anyone can praise when things go well.)
5. Religious activities. (They may or may not be signs.)

Reliable Signs of Grace

1. We experience a transformation of behavior and character. We are surprised at grace, goodness, that we did not manufacture.
2. We know a new affection for God for God's sake, not for God's gifts. We are able to love God when things don't go well, when we're depressed, when we don't have any good feelings or thoughts.

3.   We discover a new sense of knowing. This knowing is more than intel-
     lectual assent; it is a deep trust, a personal conviction. We don't have
     to browbeat others; we are able to love our enemies, particularly in our
     family and those at the other end of the political spectrum.
4.   We experience balance in our lives. We keep the Sabbath, we can play,
     we can laugh at ourselves.
5.   We know how to surrender and how to persevere. Suffering and obe-
     dience go together. Obedience is made perfect through suffering.

DUELING SPIRITS WITHIN

We intuitively know that God the Spirit animates our mind and heart and
will. Still, we can fool ourselves. We need questions from directors, friends,
the community. We pay attention to the whole sequence of an inspiration: if
a great idea brings confusion and anxiety, we may wonder where it came
from. We can tell the devils by their tails and trails. A congregation may
have a great vision and mission, but may neglect to continue listening to
God. A question may be "What is the history of this inspiration? What
effect has it had on you, the community?"

     We know joy because we are connected to God and others and the
Spirit in ourselves. We are uniquely ourselves and yet connected. We are
able to do ordinary things well. "How do we have balance between work
and prayer and play? Where are we off center?" We are humble and can
listen. We notice more and more subtle forms of compulsion and unfreedom
and hand them over to God. Our sin does not lead us to protracted neurotic
shame or despair. We don't see our enemies as all evil. We can ask ourselves, "What truth do your opponents have? What is your shadow?"

     These stages in discernment styles are broad and general. My bias is
to use the formal and complex styles for major issues like mission and divi-
sive struggles between new and old. For every day and ordinary meetings
the questions may be few. The continued asking of questions like "Where's
the call of God in this?" are cumulative and individual, and corporate listening to God is interrelated. It will seem good to the Holy Spirit and to us.

Exercises

1. Where is the next step? How do you yourself decide when it is God who speaks?

2. How does the group you're in usually discern God's will? Are the questions appropriate?

CHAPTER 6

Making and Becoming Disciples

When Jesus started teaching, his listeners knew something different was happening: "They were astonished at his teaching, for he taught them as one having authority, and not as the scribes" (Mark 1:22).

The scribes taught from the writings of those scholars who had taught before them, and they often appealed to tradition. They weighed the intellectual evidence supporting one person's opinion against that favoring another. Jesus, however, spoke as he was moved by the Spirit and not only from tradition. He spoke with the authority of one who knows a different way, one who speaks from personal knowing. He knew God intimately, loved God, knew the power of God's grace and love. Jesus' religion was firsthand; the scholars' religion was secondhand.

Jesus had a different way of teaching the disciples: "And he appointed twelve *to be with him*, and to be sent out to preach" (Mark 3:14, italics added). I believe that being with him meant living in community, learning from the experience of their life together as well as Jesus' questions and stories. Their life together was the curriculum. Jesus' perception of God was the curriculum. He taught disciples, not academics. He taught in parables, not with lectures. He encouraged his hearers to see God's hand at work in history and their own lives, the kingdom of God in their midst. He taught with the Spirit's authority.

Jesus gave himself mostly to the few who would receive the power of the Spirit most fully, but he also taught the people of the streets, ordinary people, and he took their situation into account when he spoke. He pointed out the mystery of God's presence in all creation and in them.

In most schools and in congregations, the students participate in secondhand learning, just as the scribes had in Jesus' time. I remember preaching in the first parish I served: I would look at the text, read the

commentaries, and struggle to put them together intellectually. I think about
my personal prayer time during those years: I read devotional books, but
none seemed to help me. I never recognized that I experienced God firsthand in my first parish, and I never encouraged my parishioners to refer to
their own experience of the living Christ.

One of the 20th-century's great scholars, Albert Schweitzer, who tried
to discover just what we could learn from the historical Jesus, wrote about
Jesus in his book *The Quest of the Historical Jesus.* Schweitzer ended
with this compelling paragraph about the risen Christ still teaching us:

> He comes to us as One unknown, without a name, as of old, by the
> lake-side, He came to those who knew him not. He speaks the
> same word, "Follow thou Me" and sets us to the tasks which He
> has to fulfill for our times. He commands. And to those who obey
> Him, whether they be wise or simple, He will reveal himself in the
> toils, the conflicts, the sufferings which they shall pass through in
> his fellowship, and as an ineffable mystery, they shall learn *in
> their own experience* who he is.[1]

He comes. Not "he came once." He comes in our experience. Not
secondhand. He comes as a mystery. Not just as "ideas about." We shall
learn. The process depends on our paying attention to our own lives.

My experience of education was just the opposite of what Schweitzer
describes. What the teachers graded me on was the ability to take tests and
write papers and discuss assignments in class. We were trained to be academics, with a minor in preaching. We were not encouraged to pay attention to the living Lord. Not until I stumbled into clinical pastoral education
was I encouraged to pay attention to the "living human document," the
patient with whom I visited and my own inner response to that person. Not
until then was I encouraged to notice that I did not have to bring Christ to
the suffering, that Christ was already there in their pain, and that I could
revere him there. Worshiping daily and celebrating communion on the back
wards taught me about the real presence of God in terrible situations. Later
I received a degree in spiritual formation. My most important learning grew
out of practical case studies. Where was God working in the other person?
Where was God working in me? I was taught to be open to the Spirit as I
listened. Sometimes I was open.

The Bible is clear that learning to be a Christian is different from learning to function in the world: "For the world did not know God by wisdom"

(1 Cor. 1:21). Learning to be a disciple is different from learning about God: "You are a letter of God, written not in ink but with the Spirit of the living God, not on tablets of stone but on the tablets of the human heart" (2 Cor. 3:3). Learning God's ways is different from learning the world's ways: "We impart a secret and hidden wisdom of God. . . . We impart this in words not taught by human wisdom but taught by the Spirit" (1 Cor. 2:7, 13).

Even more telling are Jesus' words to the scholars of his day: "You have your heads in the Bibles constantly because you think you'll find eternal life there. But you miss the forest for the trees. These scriptures are all about me! And here am I, standing right in front of you" (John 5:39 TM).

Jesus called the Twelve to be with him and to be disciples. He charged them to make disciples of all nations. How might we do that?

I see parallels to the biblical pattern in the writings of Parker Palmer, an educator and spiritual writer discussed in chapter 1. He makes a distinction between top-down learning and mutual learning, which he refers to as "The Objectivist Myth" and "The Community of Truth" respectively. Objectivist, top-down learning assumes that there is objective truth "out there," and that there are experts or priests or scientists who alone can train others. In the community, or mutual, model, a subject rather than an object is taught. The subject is available to be in a relationship with the learner, while an object is not.

Palmer says all real knowledge comes from this second kind of learning, with a community of people relating a subject and sharing their observations with each other. The Bible was written by people who told stories that point to the mystery in the middle of life. This model gives us a clue about how to prepare people to be disciples, both inside and outside the congregation. In some congregations, this preparation can be done very informally. The pastor can know every person, spend time with and listen to each one, and try to discern with them the growing edge of the person and the congregation.

LEARNING TO BE DISCIPLES

We can be more deliberate in our efforts to encourage this new kind of learning in the congregation, however. We might view the congregation itself—the presence of Christ in us individually and together—as the curriculum for spiritual formation. How do we learn in our life together to become disciples? Below are a number of questions congregational leaders might ask themselves when thinking about ways of growing disciples.

In Worship

Do the sermon, prayers, and hymns merely point to Christ, or do they show worshipers that Christ is in the midst of the congregation? Does the sermon point to the mystery, or does it give three points and a great quote? Are the hymns chosen to educate worshipers or to help people praise God? Are efforts made to connect private and public reading of scripture, private and corporate prayer? Are people given opportunity to think their own thoughts about the Word of God, pray their own prayers, ask for the community's prayers? Do others beside clergy lead, tell about their life? Are worshipers encouraged to pay attention to God for themselves, or does the service encourage passivity? Can all worshipers, even outsiders, understand the words of worship and the reason for doing things?

Through Mission and Ministries

What is the mission of the church? What is the focus of your life together? Making disciples? Evangelism is the beginning of mission; incorporating members is important. But what then? Are people called to know Christ in them, to look toward the hope of glory? Does your life together help people to become mature in their faith, to grow toward wholeness?

Who decides what ministries will be supported and how? Is mission just what happens "out there," or do people understand that they are involved in ministry as they go about the sometimes ordinary tasks of everyday life? How does your congregation help people to affirm their gifts and discover the ministry to which God is calling them? Do people in the congregation hear stories only about great issues and extraordinary people? Or do they hear ordinary people tell stories about being faithful in marriage, courageous when raising difficult children, a witness to God's ways when dealing with the structures of school and business?

In Committees

Do committees conduct their business like any other organization, or are they forums where community is formed? Does prayer serve as bookends for meetings, polite words at the beginning and end? Does the committee together listen for God's will? Do leaders take steps to make room for the Spirit's presence during the meeting? Are individuals invited to notice the Spirit in the meeting? Do they check in with their own stories? Can the group members discern a corporate spirit at work? Are leaders expected to grow spiritually during their term, or is it assumed that they will be burned out by the end of their duty? Does anyone ever evaluate whether there is too much busyness? Does the congregation ever "remember the Sabbath day, to keep it holy"?

Through Stewardship

Do people give to the church the same way they do to the United Fund, or are they given the opportunity to develop a sense of gratitude for God's gifts and to live from that reality? Is the church mostly concerned about members' ministry in the church, or does it provide support for their individual ministry in the world? Are people called on only when money is being raised? Or are they regularly invited in a variety of settings to talk about their needs and how the community could support them—as well as God's gifts to them and the ways they might express thanks for those gifts?

Through Education

Is the model of education mainly academic—lectures given by experts and attended by nonexperts? Is the Bible taught as an intellectual exercise? Or is education viewed as a whole-person concern? Are people helped to pay attention to God? Are they encouraged to build relationships with others in the faith community? Are they invited to show others how their relationship with God makes a difference in their life?

LEADERS AND LEARNING

We are all invited by Christ to be disciples, but some people have been called by the congregation to be leaders as well. Peter Vaill, a teacher of business leaders, talks about two kinds of education. One is institutional learning, which sets a specific goal like passing a test or being certified. It is assumed that the learner will value this goal, which is separate from the process of learning. A great volume of material must be read, and the student is expected to come up with answers to an expert's questions. An expert certifies when learning has taken place. Vaill says this type of learning is counterproductive for leaders. We live in a culture of rapid change, in "permanent white water"—an era when there can be no permanent answers. Rather, leaders must continually learn. We cannot educate leaders and then expect them to go and lead. Leading requires continual learning, and the institutional type of learning does not lead to continual learning.

Our culture demands a new kind of learning. Vaill calls this "leaderly learning." His insights have much to teach the church about being a learning organization, and leaders about learning.

1. Learning is self-directed, not originated from "experts bearing cookbooks."
2. Learning is not cramming ideas into our heads; it involves our intuition, feelings, and spirit.
3. We never become experts but must be life-long, reflective beginners.
4. Not knowing is not an occasion for shame. Asking for help and working collegially is an asset.
5. The most important kind of learning is what the person does for himself or herself.[2]

How can a congregation offer pathways for leaderly learning? I have been part of a program for leaders of congregations that offers one model.[3] A pastor, a mature Christian, or a team from within a congregation could invite lay leaders from one or more congregations to enter into a process similar to the one we conducted. Our program leaders had experience as spiritual directors, pastors, or consultants to businesses and churches.

Program participants met for three hours, every other week, during a two-year period. (Students also worked with a spiritual director who was not part of the program.) Every time we met, the students formed triads (see appendix D, handouts 6 and 7), in which they paid attention to their own spiritual life. The students also met with a mentor in a supervision group to talk about their ministry, asking the questions, Where is God in your congregation? Where is God calling you? and How are you helping others discern? The teaching curriculum covered much of the material in this book.

The community of teachers and students also prayed and entered into discernment together. We regularly asked, Where are we as a community? What are we learning? What is missing? Where is the Spirit in our life together? (See appendix D, handout 8). At times one of the students, a Quaker, led us in a Quaker process for discernment. Much of the time we used a group discernment process called dialogue. We spent time in silence. We spoke and listened to each other. We were all responsible for the educational process.

We found that this style of learning takes time. We teachers sometimes tried to teach too much too fast, and the students found it difficult to integrate their discernment with their own practice of ministry. After a while, however, our spiritual life became less an idea to talk about, and people spoke directly about discerning God individually and together. Students gradually began to ask for what they needed so they could grow. They became disciples themselves and grew to see how they could also lead others to become disciples.

A Plan for Learning

A single spiritual formation plan can be used as a starting point for a retreat with a leadership group, a weeklong conference for clergy, or a semester-long course in a congregation. The process I will describe below is similar in some ways with the program I talked about above. There is also some overlap here with the "visioning process" described in appendix A, which is designed for the whole congregation and might either precede or follow this process. Here are the core elements I would incorporate.

Set Ground Rules

Ask group members to think about a group experience in which they felt safe. Then ask, What do you need to feel safe in this group? Let the group generate its own list.

For all groups, I stress confidentiality at the beginning and at other times as appropriate. Group members might want to talk about how they understand confidentiality. The rule of thumb I work with is that they must not repeat someone else's story without that person's permission. (Confidentiality applies to pastors, too.)

I also like to give people permission not to speak. When people are given some freedom to choose how they will participate, they often are more open to joining in discussion and activities.

Develop a Learning Contract

Ask group members, What might God desire for us, as revealed in scripture? What do you want to learn? How will you and I know whether we have learned what we hoped?

Some groups want to set as a goal learning *about* spiritual formation. I explain that I will lead them through exercises in which they will *experience* spiritual formation, but that I do not plan to teach spiritual formation as a subject. Groups usually also say that their goal is to get to know one another and have an opportunity to share their individual and corporate spiritual experience. If a climate of trust and openness already exists in the group, this goal will probably be easy to reach. If the group members have worked together but have never shared at a personal level, and particularly if they do not know one another, I go very slowly and assure people that they can choose not to participate or share.

One way to learn whether something has happened through the formation process is to get feedback from others. I encourage groups that will meet for several months or longer to seek feedback from supervisors or coaches, people they serve, and colleagues. When I lead a short retreat, I ask for feedback from participants after every session. The accuracy of such feedback is usually affected by group members' feelings at the moment, so I also follow up several weeks later. The most accurate barometer is how changes are being incorporated in a person's life beginning about six months after a retreat experience.

A Process

At the beginning, I talk about spirituality, using either a written description of spirituality (appendix C, exercise 1) or the chart on different styles of knowing (fig. 2, page 10). I tell stories about my coming alive spiritually and lead them into an exercise in which they might discover how they have encountered God in their own experience.

I try to use a variety of images when asking group members to think about their experience of God: When did you move from knowing about God to worship? When were you struck with the truth that convicted and convinced you or drove you to your knees? When were you moved to tears? When was the silence deafening? When did you know that as you were doing something God was with you, in you, there in the other person? When asking group members to talk about their experience of God, it is often helpful first to let people write, then ask them to share one-on-one (see some hints in appendix C, exercise 2), and finally to share with the whole group.

Another important foundational discussion might focus on appendix D, handout 5, "How Do I Know It's God We Hear, See, and Sense?" Read Galatians 5:22, and point out that the fruits of the Spirit are attitudes, not knowledge or actions. We also "test the spirits" by sharing with others and asking them to confirm or challenge our perceptions. We may talk about the inner testimony of the Holy Spirit as we read scripture and how the difference between studying about scripture and listening to God speak to us confronts us in scripture.

Most important, I introduce "Stop, Look, and Listen" (appendix D, handout 2). Of all the things we might teach, I think this practice is central. For members of a small group to read the Bible contemplatively and to share what God is doing in their lives provides more than enough material for spiritual formation. I point out that this process summarizes many different traditions that urge us to pay attention to God. At the end of a course, students should be able to say how they know God, and they should see some change in their lives.

When working with charismatics and evangelicals, I spend more time exploring scripture. I use Luther with Lutherans (his letter to Peter the Barber) and Calvin with Reformed Christians (*A Rule for the Christian Life*). It is good to make use of theologians who wrote before the Enlightenment and who believed the Holy Spirit, not reason, is the final judge.

With people who are in 12-step groups, I talk about looking for hints of God while taking daily inventory (the 10th step). With groups that are open to Roman Catholic practice, I note that Ignatius of Loyola gave this daily *examen* or examination of consciousness a higher priority than either scripture reading or the daily office. With groups that will meet for several months, I lead some version of this experiential piece every time we meet and teach several ways of sharing reflections with each other.

Other Possibilities

Hearing God's Call. In my teaching, I often use the exercise with blind Bartimaeus and Jesus (appendix C, exercise 4) as an illustration of this new (and very old) kind of reading of scripture. This practice offers the basis for our hearing God's call both individually and collectively. In the exercise, Jesus asks us what we want, and then we ask Jesus what he desires. After we clarify this goal, then our spiritual practices can be examined. Individuals will need time for writing, sharing with others, and writing down how they will set up some support and accountability for themselves. One form of accountability might be to meet with a group, forming pairs each time the group meets to report on what each person has heard God saying.

Spiritual Types. When there is enough time, it helps groups function more smoothly to discover and compare their spiritual styles. I use Corinne Ware's book *Discovering Your Spiritual Type* and talk about the different styles and give some examples from my life. I then give Ware's test, and after group members have scored it, we put a chart on a board so that group members can compare their styles. In a congregational setting, group members might also compare their style with that of the pastor and the congregation as a whole. Many times, if the pastor has been with the congregation for a long time, he or she will have the same style as a congregation as a whole, even though there may be great variety among individuals.

We might also talk about worship, corporate and individual prayer, and education preferences for different types. Individuals might reflect on and then discuss in small groups their thoughts about:

1. Their own style, and whether they experience this exercise as an affirmation of that style.

2.   The congregation's corporate worship and education styles, and how
      to intentionally become more inclusive of other styles.
3.   Some specific hints for nurturing corporate and individual spirituality.

Discernment. When one is teaching discernment, the handout "Simple Noticing" (appendix D, handout 3) can help groups begin to notice consolation
and desolation. I probably would not use these terms, but keep the exercise
simple. A safe place to begin might be to ask people to do the exercise by
reflecting on the present awareness of the group: Are we moving with the
Spirit or against it? How do we know?

      There are many ways to augment this material. I think it is important to
soak oneself in the particular heritage of the congregation. But the most
important thing is to help people listen to God in scripture and their lives, and
to be accountable to another person or a group for discerning which of the
thoughts, feelings, and voices draw one toward God.

Learning Models for Clergy

Clergy have perhaps unique needs if they are going to become disciples
themselves and lead others into discipleship. Many clergy have been trained
in an academic atmosphere with little systematic preparation of how to be
the leader. They may nurture their own spiritual life, but it is probably not
integrated into their leadership style. They probably know how to teach
academic subjects but usually have little idea about teaching spiritual formation.

      Clergy need to learn how to discern where God calls the congregation
they serve. They need to learn to ask, What's going on and where might
God be at work in the congregation? What's going on and where might God
be at work in me? A suggested format appears in appendix D, handout 4.
Finally, they need to learn to ask, Where is God calling? What I learned
after 10 years of leading groups of clergy in such discernment is that the
clergy usually teach each other more effectively than I as the facilitator
could.

Case Studies

From that experience, I recommend that clergy arrange to meet with other like-minded seekers to reflect on the questions I noted above. At each meeting, one of the group members can present a case study about a ministry issue, and the group members can help to work through the experience using one of the many case-study processes available.[4]

Many of the clergy I know have been influenced by the late Edwin H. Friedman, a rabbi who combined his work in family systems therapy with his leadership in a congregation. Friedman said that leadership is dependent not on the information we have but on our relationship with others. Leaders do not need more ideas or technology, but need to learn how to take an emotional stance. Leaders need to be well differentiated.[5] In my experience, a case-study method gives pastors an opportunity to gain some distance on what might be a very painful situation. As they present a case, they might come to see their own overfunctioning. When the group is also centered in Christ, they may find their anxiety is lessened and they are able to detach from their feelings and their ministry.

Adaptive Leadership

Ronald A. Heifetz directs the Leadership Education Project at the John F. Kennedy School of Government at Harvard University. His book *Leadership Without Easy Answers* offers a sophisticated way of thinking about what kind of leadership is needed at a specific moment.[6] Heifetz distinguishes between three types of situations. "Technical work" involves clearly defined problems with clear solutions, and primary responsibility for completing the work rests with the leader, a person with authority. In "adaptive work" learning is required in order first to define the problem and then to identify and implement the appropriate solution. Primary responsibility for carrying out the work rests more with the person directly affected by the problem than with the leader or other authority. In some situations, both technical and adaptive work is required, and the person affected must create and implement a solution, although the person in authority might play a central role.

A few problems encountered in congregations involve technical situations with clearly definable problems and solutions that can be implemented primarily by the pastor. In many situations in the church, however, the situation is much more complex, and the pastor is powerless to make changes alone. The congregation must also take responsibility for solving the problem. For example: A new ethnic group is moving into the neighborhood, and some people from the group have started coming to church. The pastor can welcome the newcomers, pray, and preach, but much of the responsibility for ministry with the newcomers lies with the congregation itself. Finally, there are times when both technical and adaptive solutions are required, and the leader, the person with authority, and other people in the organization have to share responsibility—for example, when the congregation is preparing to launch a capital campaign for a new building program.

Heifetz's point is that all three ways of using authority can be appropriate, depending on the nature of the issue, but a rigid insistence on one method is usually not helpful. Clergy (and other congregational leaders) need to learn to negotiate the movement from an either/or style of leadership to a sophisticated understanding of authority that calls for discernment and finesse. The person with the authority in a situation does not give all the answers all the time, but neither does this leader passively refuse to give answers when they are appropriate.

Mature leaders might work through Heifetz's book, focusing especially on the kind of leadership necessary for adaptive challenges. The problem needs to be identified but not given to the community faster than people can handle it. Leaders need to avoid scapegoating or defensiveness or demonizing the opposition. It is necessary to protect the voices of leaders within the community who create temporary distress because such voices prepare the community for its move to adapt. In short, leaders need to work in a spirit of dialogue. I believe the choice of leadership style is not just an intellectual one, but one that requires spiritual discernment. This point brings us to the most important kind of learning for a pastor.

The Inner Angles

The most useful guide for clergy and other leaders that I have found comes from Eugene Peterson's book *Working the Angles*.[7] Peterson says that clergy focus on the outer elements of preaching, teaching, and administration. Without working the inner angles of listening to God in prayer, scripture, and spiritual direction, this work disintegrates into shopkeeping. Peterson explains:

The pastors of America have metamorphosed into a company of shopkeepers, and the shops they keep are churches. They are preoccupied with shopkeepers' concerns—how to keep the customers happy, how to lure customers away from competitors down the street, how to package the goods so that the customers will lay out more money. . . . The pastor's responsibility is to keep the community attentive to God. It is this responsibility that is being abandoned in spades.[8]

Peterson says that three inner acts of paying attention keep pastors doing what they are supposed to: paying attention to God in prayer, paying attention to the Word of God in scripture, and paying attention to what God is doing in individuals and the congregation as a whole.[9] My experience is that the process of learning to pay attention is a continual one, and it depends on others. If a pastor is to serve as a spiritual guide, he or she must continually find help in paying attention to God. These three dimensions described by Peterson can be learned in various ways:

1. Paying attention to God in life. At the very least, a pastor needs a friend who will listen without talking or giving advice. A triad (see appendix D, handout 7) or a skilled spiritual director can also help clergy develop the art of listening and paying attention to God. Students I have worked with in doctor of ministry programs say this listening is the most important thing they have done for their ministry.
2. Paying attention to God in scripture. At the least, a pastor needs to be part of a Bible study group that moves past the academic to contemplative Bible study. My experience is that study groups easily disintegrate into an academic exercise or a practical seminar about preaching the text. Someone needs to act as convener, and the group needs to take inventory and regularly ask, How are we spending our time?
3. Paying attention to God in the other, the congregation. At the least, a pastor can talk with other pastors about what is happening in the congregation. At the most, a group moderated by an outsider may help pastors discern where God is at work in their congregations, and where they might be stuck themselves (see appendix D, handout 4).

Forming a Group

Groups such as those I have been describing can be formed in many ways. Perhaps the most successful ones are created informally as pastors risk sharing their struggles and propose to others that they enter into a disciplined growth process together. Gatherings might be built into judicatory meetings. People sometimes reach across denominational lines and covenant to meet regularly to study, pray, attend to each others' wounds, and help each other in discernment. Seminaries and church-related colleges, health-care centers, and other institutions serving a wide geographic area might sponsor a gathering for congregational leaders—clergy, lay leaders, or both. I will be with a team teaching a two-year leadership program for pastors in my denomination who come from all over the Midwest. Some spiritual friends use e-mail, while many coaches rely almost exclusively on the telephone. A good way to begin forming a group is to ask Jesus for help and pay attention to the doors that open.

GO, MAKE DISCIPLES

I believe Jesus commands us to make disciples to remind us what is central in a congregation. Our central business is forming disciples and learners. The path is something like the five stages of growth I have mentioned, and Jesus describes the goal: "Abide in me and I in you" (John 15:4). Disciples will grow at different rates and in different directions and will develop different styles. In every case, however, the learning of individuals, groups, and the congregation as a whole are interrelated. Their spiritual formation is not the sole responsibility of clergy, an adult education group, or a spirituality task force. Rather, it is the responsibility of all the congregation's leaders to help individuals learn to pay attention to God. In order to do this, they must themselves be in the process themselves of learning to listen to God—alone and with others. I end where I began: "Today, if you hear God's voice, do not harden your hearts" (Ps. 95:7). "Give your entire attention to what God is doing right now" (Matt. 6:33, TM).

Exercises

1. What will you do to make disciples, teaching them?

2. How will the clergy learn to see that their own spiritual growth in awareness is important to the congregation?

3. How will leaders learn leaderly rather than academic ways?

4. How will the system and culture of the whole congregation help form us in the image of Jesus Christ?

APPENDIX A

Discernment in the "Visioning Process"

Jonna Fantz

Jonna Fantz, author of appendixes A and B, has been an English teacher, is a poet, and has taught the material in "Stop, Look, and Listen" (see appendix B). Tom Allen is a management consultant for corporations, municipalities, and congregations. Allen, Fantz, and I designed the material for developing a mission statement. The material includes a standard process designed with stage 3 churches in mind (see chapter 2), as well as suggestions about simplifying the process for churches that are in turmoil, congregations that have never undergone such a process, and churches that are heavily dependent on clergy for leadership.

In recent years the emphasis of the church-administration world has been on the process of developing a vision and an accompanying mission statement. Many books graph the suggested processes. Defining themselves has become an important tool for churches. Most processes, by and large, have been copied from the business world with little or no modification. A few have come from Quaker or Jesuit traditions. Business models have worked successfully for many churches, because the church is an organization with similarities to other organizations. However, the church is also a unique organization. The church lives in relationship to God in a unique way. It claims to be the body of Christ, more intimately connected to God than are secular organizations. In fact, many secular groups are more open to listening to the Spirit than most churches. The church needs to listen for God to speak and guide, and to use methods that reflect members' relationship with God.

With these observations in mind, the process of discerning a vision and a mission is vital. This may be a life-giving process for a congregation, offering tremendous focus and insight into its unique call and what God has given it. Working as a team, a spiritual director and a business systems analyst have developed a process that combines listening to God with contemporary business practice. The process outlined below is a simple process that most churches can work through. After the basic process, a simplified version is described, for use in smaller congregations, congregations that already have a vision statement but have new leadership, or congregations accustomed to the clergy taking most of the leadership functions. These differences do not distinguish beginning or advanced churches. It is mostly a choice of how much time and energy to invest in the process. Then, a few more steps are offered for congregations with some experience in the area of spiritual formation that would like to make the process more encompassing.

BASIC DISCERNMENT IN DEVELOPING A VISION STATEMENT

Primarily two movements will occur in this process. The first is the important step of learning to listen to God, opening our corporate ears to what God may be saying to us. The second is the process of developing a vision statement and implementing it.

Moving your congregation into a deeper, more focused kind of listening may be an amazing journey. The question is always where to start. The suggestions in chapter 4 or in the bibliography may help. Sermons are essential, as well as people's sharing of their individual stories. Asking boards and committees first to check in and then to say where they have noticed God is a good place for working groups to begin. Allow plenty of time for members of your congregation to try out this new way of relating to God. As individuals begin to experience talking more openly about their relationship with God, they will need a community to help them to sort through those experiences and discern what is God's voice and presence in each person's thoughts, fears, and desires. Through hearing God and each other, we begin to discern God's will as part of the ordinary life of the church.

To determine what type of process you should use, it will be helpful to evaluate your church. The first model we present is the basic model. All other models are modifications of this one. The basic model is best used in a church with an empowered laity that makes decisions with the support and guidance of the staff. These leaders are frequently found in churches that have a predominance of baby boomers. They are comfortable working alongside staff and have a clear understanding of the importance of lay leadership. A team of lay leaders can suitably facilitate this process. There are four major steps in this model.

BASIC MODEL

Step 1

Enlist all who will to commit themselves to a two-week program of prayerfully reading a scripture passage every day about the church and writing down what is learned. These people will be asked to spend a Saturday morning together at the end of the program to share what they have found. Make a list of appropriate passages for the two weeks and ask the volunteers who will commit themselves to this study to come forward for a blessing. Give the references for the whole congregation. Ask them to read especially Matthew 28:19-20. Request that people ask, as they read, what Jesus says for us today. Are we in the disciple-making business, or social action, or worship? The two main questions that become the focus during these intensive two weeks of study are:

- What have you noticed God saying in this scripture?
- Where is God calling us as a church?

For the Sunday morning worship services, the sermon texts should be drawn from this list, with everyone invited to listen to God's intention. It would be good for the pastor to be clear about his or her beliefs, but also to clarify other possibilities. Are you in the business of disciple-making or providing inspiring worship or doing social action? Let the whole life of the church focus in on these scriptures for two weeks. Encourage the youth programs, small groups, Sunday school classes, and Bible studies to devote themselves for two weeks to reading stories and praying for guidance.

Step 2

On a Saturday morning after this intense two-week listening process, bring together those who have read the texts to begin to share what they have heard. Divide the people into groups of six. Ask one person in each group to write down ideas on a flip chart as each person shares where he or she noticed God. Each person should be given a block of time to share—say, three to five minutes. During that time everyone should listen carefully. The rest of the group may ask questions for clarification, but should save their opinions until it is their own time to speak. After everyone has spoken, the group facilitator may allow for a general discussion. During this process, trust that God has spoken to each person through the last two weeks, and pay attention to what God has said through them. The person who records the information (perhaps just the main themes) should be quick to repeat back to the speaker what has been heard, and to check for accuracy. This really is a process of each person's sharing his or story from the past two weeks.

When people's stories seem to connect or a theme emerges, this point should be noted by circling or underlining the repeated words, images, and phrases. Connections can begin to be made at this small-group level. Then a shift may take place. People may begin noticing how this congregation does what God asks. People may be able to write general statements of accomplishment such as: "We are a friendly church. We care for social justice. Our liturgy helps us enter God's presence. Our people grow spiritually."

The second question, "Where do you think God is calling this church?" can be dealt with simultaneously or separately from the first question. Often from the stories people share, they will draw conclusions about where God is leading them. Make sure that all sharing and questions center on these two questions. Whether you deal with them together or separately is less important.

The pastor should try to drift around to each group and listen in on the process. The pastor may offer encouragement if needed. Eventually he or she may want to sit down with one group and listen to what is being discussed in depth—but without comment.

When this process has been completed, the whole group should gather again to share the full results. This is an opportune time for the pastor to share what he or she has heard and seen in the past two weeks, in scripture and in the small groups. As all the stories are compiled, try to sort them around certain themes. You may hear that God is calling your church to evangelism, outreach, spirituality, social justice, or children's ministry. Be constantly listening for the emergence of a direction that seems to be repeated again and again in the dialogue. It may be appropriate to pause for silent reflection, or the group may be so busy and energized that the process will flow. Include singing or praying aloud when appropriate, for this is a work of the Spirit. The mood should be one of worship as God makes himself known.

After the responses have been arranged by theme, the entire group needs to choose which of the themes seem the most compelling. This is an appropriate time for silent prayer or a quiet hymn that asks for guidance. After this, ask people to vote for the priorities to which they are guided. One method is to give each person three dot stickers and have each prayerfully place them next to the themes that seem to him or her the most important. Most likely, three or four themes will emerge. Talk about them to see whether general agreement emerges. If no clear pattern develops, perhaps you could have the whole group work as a dialogue, asking people to pray and state what they feel the Spirit is saying to them. It may be that this part of the process is not conclusive. The church board may take up this task and decide whether it can make a statement or whether the congregation needs more study. Why is there a lack of clarity? Does it stem from conflict or divergent points of view? Has the pastor not made herself clear? Is scripture not clear? Is the parish grappling with issues of congregational identity or culture? Make sure to end this voting time with thanksgiving, no matter what happens. If no clarity emerges, ask for help from God and an outsider.

The pastor and other leaders should share from the pulpit the results from the Saturday gathering. The whole congregation is invited to participate again in listening and praying about what the church understands as direction from God. An invitation should be issued to everyone to come the following Saturday and to work on the vision statement.

Step 3

On the following Saturday begin the process of shaping the vision into a statement. This task should be done in a small group. The members of this group should be given the main themes that emerged at the end of the last week's meeting. There may be no perceptible order to begin with, but a consensus should emerge. Begin by inviting participants into a time of prayer. Read the themes aloud, and ask the group to utter short prayers about these themes together. If any verses emerged as key passages for the church, share those as well. It may be good to finish this prayer time by singing some familiar hymns or choruses.

Staying in this worshipful tone, begin to draw these themes together in a coherent sentence and paragraph. Ideally, it will be a paragraph short enough to be memorized, with a maximum of four points. Invite people to listen carefully to each other and to God. Leave space for silence and prayer. A chart should be readily available to all, and all members of the group should have pencils and paper for jotting down their thoughts. Keep the process slow. Let people wrestle with word choices and the syntax of the sentence. If arguments arise, have people repeat what the person who spoke last has said and then add their own insights. This strategy will encourage people to listen carefully to one another. It may be good to call for prayer frequently— prayers of thanksgiving and supplication. One person may be named as group process observer to give feedback on where the Spirit is working and where the process seems to be stuck.

When the group has finally completed the vision statement, or the group is exhausted—whichever comes first—everyone should write the statement down, take it home, and continue to pray.

Step 4

The pastor and lay leaders should share the vision statement with the congregation in a sermon and service. Stories from the small-group time on Saturday should be told. The person acting as small-group process observer may select three or four small-group participants who symbolize the group process. Announce that at the end of this service, another meeting will convene to receive feedback. Have copies of the statement on hand for people to take home and pray about.

At this point if there is clarity and enthusiasm, you may proceed to what are usually called "goals and objectives." Meet one last time with those who are willing from the congregation and again break the large group into smaller groups. Three questions should be asked of these small groups as they think about this new statement of their purpose:

(a) What are the next steps for the church to take?
(b) What evaluation process is used to make sure that we remain faithful to this vision? This step need not be elaborate, but the congregation might evaluate itself at the time of the annual meeting. See the suggestions later in the text.
(c) How are we growing disciples, mature Christians?

Again invite careful listening and prayer as the groups begin to work on the specifics of what God is calling them to. These questions could be written on flip charts and then shared with the larger group as a whole. Remember that this occasion may mark the beginning of an ongoing process of seeing the church define itself differently. After this, the various committees and organizations will be asked to carry on this conversation about their ministries. The danger is that this mission statement will be dropped. It will become another piece of paper that has been shelved. The way to prevent such an outcome is through an ongoing evaluation process. Two forms of evaluation will be needed.

The first is for the church to use the vision statement as an evaluation of its own ministry in its community. Say that the congregation has decided that its first mission is to make disciples of all nations. How is the congregation as a whole fulfilling this vision? What about budget, time, and energy? What about individuals? Are individuals intentionally listening to the Lord? Staff members should evaluate their ministries in the church according to the vision statement. In an evaluation of how the year has gone, each area of ministry should constantly look back to the vision statement, which becomes the central anchor to which everything in the church's schedule is moored. When decisions are being made in governing board meetings, the vision should provide a place from which to begin. This statement becomes what we know God is calling us to in all situations and can help clarify what God is calling us to in a specific situation.

Second, the church will also need to evaluate the vision itself. If the church discovers that the call of God is changing with the congregation and the circumstances surrounding the church, then the vision statement should change as well. When a new group of leaders is elected, none of whom went through the process, then a renewal of the vision should take place. The statement should remain current with the church's understanding of its identity and where it is being called. A process similar to the one described should be embarked upon every two or three years, in which the church asks itself again: Why are we here? What is God doing? Where is God calling? This process should be built into the church calendar so that it becomes a part of the church's culture. Ideally, the statement should be evaluated and fine-tuned yearly.

This four-step process may be modified to fit your church's interests and needs. It provides a solid basis from which to launch the process of corporate discernment. Once having been through this task, you may discover that this way of doing business in the church is so dynamic and powerful that it begins to guide other decisions you make. Budget planning, staff changes, building programs, and so forth can all be done through a process similar to this one in which we pause to hear what God has to say first, in the midst of the process, and always. It transforms the process of making business decisions into an act of worship.

THE LEADERSHIP-DRIVEN MODEL

If your church is more leadership-driven, more dependent on clergy, the previous model may be too much of a stretch for your laity. A congregation that has just begun or has recently been through an exhausting transition may need to have the clergy take a more directive role. Sometimes the generation a congregation serves makes a difference as well. The basic model works well with a baby-boomer congregation, whereas a parish dominated by members in their 60s, 70s, and 80s tends to want a more pastor-led model. If this is the case for your congregation, the four steps listed in the basic model can be modified to a more pastor-led focus.

Note that the pastoral focus is important. The pastor and board will first need to learn to listen to God in some of the ways that we encouraged the whole church to listen to God. Of course, this will change the church naturally, because as leaders move into listening, that action will transform their ministries and relationships. If the leadership is committed to personal spiritual formation, it will be ready to listen to God for the congregation as a whole.

The steps will be similar for this process, except that the work will most likely be done in a small group and then shared with the congregation. This group could include the pastoral staff, the governing board, and various lay leaders. In a large congregation, this would be a sizable group, which more than likely can afford a consultant to help with the process.

Step 1

Begin with worship and hand out a text like Acts 15 ahead of time for members to study, pray with, and write notes about.

The pastor can focus his or her sermons on these verses and ask these important questions at the congregational level. Focus on Jesus' command to make disciples and on Acts 15. Encourage the people to write down any input they might have on this topic.

Step 2

As with the basic model, bring the group together. The pastor may do some teaching about the nature of the church. Begin with prayer and worship, perhaps using Matthew 28; then move into sharing ideas. Someone may record these on flip charts and note themes. Remember that prayer and silent reflection are key to making space for God to speak. Remember to leave time for each person in the group to speak. Consider carefully what each says, and ask questions.

Then begin to prioritize and group the comments under themes. Try to come up with several themes that capture what the group is hearing and seeing. Make sure that everyone in the group takes these themes away to pray about until your next meeting.

Step 3

This step should be the same as in the basic model. Begin with worship; then using the themes, craft a sentence or paragraph that states your vision.

Again, let this be a time of wrestling with clarity and focus. Listen carefully to each other. If need be, have people repeat what the previous speaker said before adding their own contribution. Pray often. Soak in silence. Be willing to wait for the vision God is sharing to emerge. Don't jump too quickly to consensus. The pastor may actively guide the process and persuade the congregation to accept the vision. Many congregations expect the pastor to give the direction. The congregation will be presented with the vision and asked for feedback.

Step 4

Again address the three questions that were addressed in the basic model with the same small group:

(a) What are the next steps for the church to take? The pastor may begin with suggestions. What does this mean for your Sunday school class, for your committee, for your volunteer position?
(b) What evaluation process is used to make sure that we are being faithful to this vision?
(c) Are we growing disciples, mature Christians?

Remember, the evaluation question, especially, should be addressed carefully. Evaluation will be a powerful way for this vision statement to become a part of the church culture.

After this final step, the whole congregation should be notified of the decisions made by its leadership. Invite congregational feedback and input. Preach a series on this vision statement, talking about the dreams that the leadership has for the church. Find places in the church to post the vision statement. Use it as part of worship. Make sure that congregational members have copies. Encourage congregational ownership by asking the leaders to begin to think through the mission statement and its impact on the church.

FOR THOSE WHO WANT TO INVEST MORE TIME

Many more steps are possible besides those outlined in the basic model. These other steps can be used to make the process more encompassing. The use of these steps will be determined by several variables.

First is the pastor's journey in spiritual development. If the pastor and a good share of the other leaders are experienced in listening to God, the congregation may be ready for a more contemplative model. There are several Quaker and Jesuit-inspired models.

Second is the journey of the church as a whole. Does the church listen well to outsiders? Is there openness to change? Is the congregation ready to face its dark side without defensive frustration? With these questions in mind, read through the following tools, selecting whichever ones may be helpful, and add them to the basic model.

It is possible to invite the congregation to form small groups at the time of the annual meeting. People will be asked two questions:

1. Where have you known God at work in the congregation?
2. Where do you think God is calling us?

Obviously, there will be preparation ahead of time with sermons and laypeople sharing their observations as examples. Afterward, the responses will be clustered into themes and put in order of priority, according to the number who mentioned each theme. Then the board will study, pray, and report back.

Fasting and Listening Prayer

Through the centuries abstaining from food for times of prayer has been one way of helping people move into deeper communion with God. Calling an entire body of believers into fasting can have a transforming effect on a congregation as it goes through the shared experience of seeking God through self-denial. The value depends on the readiness of a congregation to embark on this journey.

Listening prayer invites the person praying to be silent so that God may speak. Silence or centering or recollection means being quiet outwardly and inwardly to listen for God's voice. There are many ways in which the congregation can be invited to participate in listening prayer during worship. Listening prayer is a powerful way to help open the ears of a congregation.

Historical Timeline

This project can result in a powerful visual display of the life of the church as it intersects with people's lives. Draw out a time line from the founding of the church to the present. Mark on the time line events in the life of the church deemed by members to be significant. Be honest, including both times of prosperity and times of struggle. Note significant changes, controversies, and staff changes. Include building projects, growth surges, the beginnings and endings of programs. Leave plenty of space between these events on the time line so that individuals can add their personal memories.

Next, invite people to write in the date they joined the church. This will help give them a history of the church as well as showing when they entered into that history. If you have enough space and time, people can record other significant events that happened in their life with the church—baptism, confirmation, marriage, ministry, and so forth. Some may want to record world events. Give people plenty of time to look over the time line, familiarizing themselves with the church's origins. Help them also to gain perspective on their contributions to the church as they notice where other people have participated.

Make time after this for people to share what insights they gained in seeing this time line. Note if people have seen recurring themes in the church's past. Be open to prayers of repentance, thanksgiving, and intercession on behalf of the church.

Interview—External Environment

People from the congregation know the truth they see about the church. Those who are not in the congregation offer another view of the truth. The more of the truth the church has about itself, the more it will be able to hear what God is saying. As various members of a congregation go out into the community and interview people about the church, their eyes will be opened to misunderstandings, insights, and unique perspectives that were missing from their understanding. It is good to interview neighbors and community members and former members. Two questions are especially helpful to ask in these interviews:

1. In what areas do you think that people in our neighborhood struggle or have needs?
2. What do you think of our church? What do you know about how people in the community view us?

Questions should be preceded by conversation and asked in a way that they make sense. For instance, neighbors can be asked whether the church is a good neighbor. Make it easy for people to respond, and use the interview as an opportunity for people to have a positive experience with the church. Sometimes the perception of the community will seem at odds with what the church knows to be true about itself. This is a key moment in trying to learn what God is revealing to us about ourselves. Being able to accept what others tell us about ourselves will open us to what God is telling us about ourselves as well. The material should be shared in a small group and written up for sharing with the congregation.

Dialogue with People in the External Environment

In the Bible, it is frequently the outsiders who bring some new awareness to the people of God. Jesus says that not in all of Israel has he seen faith like that of the Roman centurion. It is the publican who prays, "Lord have mercy on me." Jesus says the publican is closer to God than the so-called spiritually advanced Pharisee. And it is the Gentiles whom God uses to open up the church. In Acts, Peter has a vision of unclean animals as a sign that God wants the church to open up.

What group might this be in a local situation? It could be gay couples moving into the area, or a neighborhood group of activists who oppose the church's sponsorship of a Boy Scout troop. The group that is feared might be a charismatic or fundamentalist group in the community. It might be new people who are coming into the church from a different culture. The church leaders might hear complaints, but what if the congregation were to believe that God was knocking on the door, just as God did with the Gentiles? Then the church might try to use a form of dialogue with the other group.

The others could be invited as a group to have coffee. After a superficial meeting, if there is trust, a core group of the outsiders and insiders might be invited to meet with a facilitator. The theme might be "Where I See Community." What happened in Acts 15, among other things, is that people shared their stories of working with outsiders. The church expanded its viewpoints of how God was working.

There are times to bring in an outside helper. Just to have a somewhat neutral presence may help leaders hear about the church in a new way. The pastor may have been voicing certain truths for years, but an outsider is usually listened to with fresh ears. An outsider who is a veteran at working with groups may guide the experience with less anxiety, a more detached point of view. The outsider may be able to notice the atmosphere, attitudes, and eccentricities that an insider doesn't. The pastor and leaders usually have a special appreciation for a consultant.

Excellent and detailed books on managing change are available. Three of them are *Leading Change in the Congregation*, by Gilbert Rendle; *Leading Change*, by John Kotter; and *The Corporate Culture Survival Guide*, by Edgar Schein (see bibliography). A sense of God's call, skill in management, and a trust in the Spirit to guide are all part of the process.

Stop, Look, and Listen

Jonna Fantz

Individuals often experience a movement deeper into relationship with God. Old disciplines feel dry, and old images of God don't fit anymore. A new hunger for God draws a person into a more intimate relationship. This often life-changing process can be exciting and frightening. A spiritual director can help provide guidance and support through this significant change. But what happens when a church begins this growth process? How does one nurture and encourage this growth on a congregationwide scale as well as provide spiritual direction? As the church in the 21st century becomes more aware of spiritual formation, this question is being raised increasingly in all sorts of churches, from liberal to conservative, urban to rural, "mega" to "house."

It is because of this question that a group of people gathered to work on this curriculum. Two spiritual directors, a seminary student, a curriculum developer, and an editor pulled together materials that would give people a place to begin. The "Stop, Look, and Listen" curriculum is the result of their joint efforts. This curriculum packet gives people some beginning tools in learning to listen for the voice of God. It raises important discernment questions, and it offers some new disciplines that can give a congregation some new territory to explore.

Included in the materials are the following pieces:

1. A storytelling chapter that will guide people through a process of telling and listening to the stories in and around them.
2. A leader's guide for taking people through a six-week course on the fundamentals of learning to listen to Jesus. Handouts for these sessions are included.

3. A participant's guide that provides space for participants in the "Stop, Look, and Listen" course to practice what they are learning on their own between group sessions.
4. A series of six sermons that reinforce what is happening in the sessions each week. These may be used simply as suggestions.
5. Extra teaching and helpful tips for leaders who will guide these sessions.
6. An individualized guide to help people walk through the sessions on their own if they are unable to participate in the group sessions.

In each week of the course, not only are different disciplines learned, but also a different focus emerges. This combination of topical study and exploration of spiritual disciplines makes for a powerful learning experience. For the first week "Gratitude" is the focus, with a daily examination in which each individual begins to learn to look through the moments of his or her life for the gifts that God is giving.

The second week focuses on "Our Heart's Desire." This week people pray honestly what is in their heart and listen for God's reply. This invites a process of purification that leads our desires into unity with God's.

In the third week we focus on "Listening to God With Your Heart." This unit explains a new way to read scripture that focuses on the message that God wants to apply to our lives right now.

The fourth week's segment considers the following process: "Discerning if It's God We Hear." We study the fundamental inner movements toward God and away from God, learning what those movements are like as well as wise ways to respond to them.

In the fifth week we begin to explore "A Regular Practice." Participants will listen for God to guide them into a regular meeting time and into disciplines to practice.

The final week focuses on "Support." This chapter deals with ensuring that what has been learned and practiced in this class will bring lasting change in the lives of the participants.

If you have questions, write to John Ackerman, 2833 East Lake of the Isles Parkway, Minneapolis, MN 55408, call (612) 871-6377, or send an e-mail message to ackerman@visi.com.

Four Exercises for Groups and Churches

I have used four exercises again and again. When I start working with a church leadership group, I employ some version of these. I use them in seminary classes and in workshops. These exercises make a good retreat activity, but they could also be used once a month at a regular meeting. My practice is to begin with some version of these when I engage in individual spiritual direction. For groups I alternate between doing an exercise for individuals and then doing it for the group. I have *italicized* my directions to the group.

Exercise 1:
Where Have You Known Grace, God, the Mysterious Presence?

With groups unaccustomed to silence, I might begin with some music, or read a psalm about God's saving activity. I'd talk about silence and singing as ways that we can stop thinking about things and know at a deeper level. I would cite the historical role of the Bible telling the story of God's action, and point out that we can tell the history of our own actions. With groups that are used to a little silence, I would start with silence. With people who are uncomfortable with God-talk, I'd talk about grace, "centering," wonder, and love. With evangelicals and charismatics, I'd talk about the Holy Spirit in their lives. Ask people to close their eyes and focus on their breathing, but give them permission not to do this, and even not to participate in the exercise.

Here are the words I use. Leave long pauses between the words.

- *Let your chair support you, remembering that underneath are the everlasting arms.*
- *Focus on your breath, and let it be a prayer.*
- *Breathe out, letting go.*
- *Breathe in the breath of God.*
- *See if you can remember a time when God seemed real, either in church or outside. Just let some event arise from your memory when you felt centered, or had a sense of awe, or were at home, or loved.*
- *Can you re-enter this time in your memory?*
- *What did you sense, feel, think?*
- *Who was there?*
- *Was God there?*
- *How did you know?*

(Allow time for people to remember in silence.)

- *Take a moment to write this down, if you'd like to. It may help you to be more specific, more concrete.*

(Allow more time.)

Share Your Story with the Group

"I'd like to share what I remembered." Serve as a model for the group by sharing your own story. Tell people that we have different stories and different ways or languages of experiencing God. Invite people to tell what has happened. If this is a large group or a very introverted group, break into small groups of two or three. Give permission for people not to share. When you are in a group, after each person speaks, affirm him or her. Many people have never talked to others about their faith story and need encouragement.

Instruct listeners to avoid discussion or arguments. Simply listen, for you are on holy ground.

At the end, ask about the exercise. *What was helpful? What wasn't? What have we learned from each other?* (You will get important information about the group soul. Do they trust enough to share? Are they afraid of New Age or evangelical language?) For the group as a whole: Start the same way. Adjust to the needs of the group.

- *Now I'd like to ask you to go back in your memory and think about the history of this congregation.*
- *What were the times when you felt at home, as though you were a part of something big?*
- *When were you filled with delight or awe or compassion? Could it be that the Spirit of God was in these things?* [Pause]
- *Is it while singing or during communion or at the time of the sermon that you have a sense of God's presence?*

Again, divide participants into small groups if they are unaccustomed to such conversation, or are more introverted. With a working group it may be helpful to start talking about the Spirit. But again, give people permission not to talk, to take a pass, to listen. To avoid putting people on the spot, I recommend not going sequentially around the circle but hearing from those who volunteer to speak.

At the end say that the group has begun doing discernment, paying attention to where God is. What was it like to remember and share?

EXERCISE 2:
DAILY INVENTORY

Just as we can remember God in the past, so also we can become aware daily, even moment to moment, of God's will, desire, plan.

- *Close your eyes, please, and focus on your breathing. Let your body be relaxed. The Lord is my shepherd, I shall not want. He maketh me to lie down in green pastures. Can you let Jesus lead you, to give you what he wants to give in this exercise? Pray for eyes to see, ears to hear.*
- *Go back over the last 24 hours. Is there something that comes to your attention? What is it?* [long pause] *Go back into the event just for a moment. What might it be saying? Is your response that of gratitude, or is a different prayer called for? What is your prayer?* [Pause so that participants can pray.] *Now, can you just be with God for a minute, perhaps in the green pasture, beside the still waters.* [Again, pause.]
- *Now take a moment to write down what you noticed.*

- *Then share with a partner, if you care to. Here is some advice: Try to avoid giving advice to the people you listen to. Affirm what seems to be of God. Ask questions to lead to more awareness: This "nothing" that you remember—could God be in the ordinary, in the absence?*

Then move into groups. With the group:

- *Where has the Spirit been as we have been sharing?*
- *Where is there a resonance within you as others shared?*
- *Was there a sense of belonging?*

With the group:

- *Let's be still a moment, and ask the Spirit to guide us, teach us.*
- *Let's go back over the meeting. Where were we working with the Spirit, listening to God and each other?*
- *When did it seem that we were connected?*
- *Were these moments anything like the time you went back in history and remembered God's touch with you individually, or remembered God's gifts and presence with us together?*

This exercise depends on the trust and history of the group. I probably wouldn't tie in the individual and group experience of the Spirit at first. But with experienced groups, doing so can be powerful when the group suddenly becomes aware of the Spirit working though us individually and together.

EXERCISE 3:
SCRIPTURE

Take a passage of scripture like Matthew 25: "Go, make disciples of all nations." Tell the group that we will do a different kind of Bible study. We'll take this as a personal word from God. We'll listen not only for ideas, but for God's heart, God's passion for us.

Begin with a prayer, using whatever pattern of silence, breath, scripture, and prayer for inspiration seems to fit the group.

Read the first time, and ask people what they think *[long pause]*.

Read again, and ask people what they feel, what word or phrase resonates within *[another pause]*.

Read again, and ask people to respond in a prayer (silently—unless this is a trusting or extroverted group) *[silence]*.

Read again, and ask people to respond nonverbally to God. You may pray this old prayer:

> O God of Peace, who hast taught us that in returning and rest we shall be saved, in quietness and confidence shall be our strength. Lift us, we pray thee, into thy presence, where we may be still and know that thou art God.

Let participants make notes, and again share your response. Then ask the group to share, perhaps one-on-one.

With a group or congregational focus, you can use a scripture passage for the group as a whole. It depends on where the church is, in emotionally trusting the community with feelings and spiritual stories. If it is wounded, take five minutes after silence and reading the scripture, and have members imagine the congregation as a man by the pool at Bethesda. Then ask, "What does Jesus say? Jesus asks us if we want to be healed. Do we?" If the group is confused, work with a passage in which Jesus sends the disciples out. If your church is too busy, let the congregation be Martha in the story of Mary and Martha. What does Jesus say to the church when it's like Mary? When it's a Martha?

EXERCISE 4:
JESUS CALLS US

I start by saying that God calls us not only vocationally, but also in our daily walk. I prepare people with music or prayer or silence to hear God's word to us. I read the story of blind Bartimaeus (Luke 18:35-43). Sometimes I stop at the end of Jesus' question: "What do you want me to do for you?"

Then I suggest that people give Jesus their answer. What do they need now? Healing? Opening and listening? Guidance? What is their prayer, at the deepest part of their heart?

Then suggest that they turn the question around. What does Jesus want, desire for them? How does Jesus seem? What is Jesus calling them to? Write a response if you can.

Write. Share one-on-one. Have a brief discussion. What is it like not to know? Can they simply be? Can they let the Spirit pray in them with sighs too deep for words?

Then suggest that they tell Jesus what they want for this group, the church. What does Jesus say? Write. Share.

Put both responses on paper.

The church may tell all sorts of stories about God in its midst. The annual meeting may collect these yearly. The governing board may collect stories monthly and talk about the most revealing ones. Then when tragedy comes, members are used to discerning God's call.

Every committee may begin by asking where God has been. It may end by asking where the Spirit has been. Then it becomes easier to read scripture and to hear God's call in the mixture of scripture and life. Individuals may find themselves hearing God.

Handouts

This appendix includes handouts that may be used independently of the rest of the book. Many of them are referred to in the sample spiritual development process described in chapter 6.

1. "Spiritual Formation" offers my definition of some of the basic terms. I think it is important for people to wrestle with whatever definition is given, so that there is more than a surface agreement about these terms.

2. "Stop, Look, and Listen" is a guide to reading scripture contemplatively and listening to God in one's life. The practice forms a basic daily discipline for many people. The emphasis is not on doing it right, but on listening to God. Those who follow this practice need to hold themselves accountable to someone who helps them ask, What is God saying, and what will you do about it? I teach this process together with the triad groups as the basic daily listening exercise.

   To teach people who are not experienced, begin with a group meditation focusing on things we are and are not grateful for (see appendix C, exercise 2). There are many forms of teaching how to read the Bible contemplatively, and in appendix C, exercises 3 and 4, I suggest two classic patterns.

3. "Simple Noticing." As we learn discernment, we begin noticing the direction in which our inner thoughts, movements, and feelings take us. The process can be difficult for people who never notice what is happening inside. It is particularly difficult for some to engage in self-examination and personal reflection when they are stuck in guilt, shame,

addictions, anger, or grief. These people need to focus on God's love. The practice can be done in groups, including in worship. This pattern of offering thanks for blessings and asking for help is one of the basic patterns of the psalms.

4.   "Noticing in the Congregation." The exercise outlined in 3, above, and this one are complementary. The leader or facilitator of a group might ask the questions: Where is God in this situation? In what direction are we going? What is the call of God in this situation?

5.   "How Do I Know It's God We See, Hear, and Sense?" The five statements in this handout are classic criteria for discernment. I think it is also important for people and groups to learn a brief form of these criteria that they can reflect on in situations throughout the day.

6.   "Peer Group Format for Case Study." One person needs to act as a timekeeper for this case study process to work. The discipline of keeping time protects groups from "analysis paralysis," and the times for prayer help members discern God's activity.

7.   "Triads" are one way to help people learn how to listen. What makes this approach unique is asking that the speakers talk about their experience of God (which rarely happens in casual conversation), and the listener listens without trying to "fix" the other. Most people find the observer position the most difficult. It takes many groups three to five meetings to feel comfortable with triads.

8.   "Dialogue" as a formal practice is widely described, but in my experience, groups need a facilitator to help them do this.

Spiritual Formation

Spirituality is a new name for a vitally important foundation of our Christian lives. The old name is "piety." Since the 1960s it has often been divorced from religion. Spirituality is our relationship to God, others, and ourselves. Religion is the outer structure of ideas, dogmas, worship, and organization.

We might think of Christian spirituality as *paying attention to* God: listening and learning from the risen Christ through the Holy Spirit in us and among us. We respond to God by living out God's love, call, will, desire, and passion in all areas of our life.

Spiritual formation is the process whereby we grow in our ability to pay attention, the way we help form what God is doing. It involves all the ways we are being formed in the image of Christ in our inner life and outer ministry. Spiritual formation is the congregation growing in its ability to learn from God, to grow toward becoming a community like the Trinity.

Stop, Look, and Listen
A Way of Listening to God

Stop: *Breathe out and in. (Or walk, listen to music, etc.)*
Pay attention to your breath. Let go, let the Spirit breathe into you.

Look: *At the past 24 hours and your reaction.*
What is there to thank God for?
What are you not grateful for?
What internal messages were going around in your head?
Say I'm sorry about hurting someone else?
Hand over my internal messages that are self-punitive?
Ask for others?
What is your heart's desire? What grace do you need?
What is missing? You want _____ so that _____.

Listen: *To the Word of God in scripture, spoken to you today.*
Read aloud.
What shimmers, stands out?
How does it address your longing?
Pray briefly and in a heartfelt way.
Let yourself rest in the goodness of God.
How might you receive the Word today?
Respond. Is there something to think? Do? Be?
Write a few notes to yourself so that you don't forget.

"Look" is a version of a daily *examen* or examination of conscience. "Listen" is a form of *lectio divina*, spiritual reading.

Simple Noticing

For the sake of simplicity, let us look at two movements of the soul: toward God and away from God. Let us assume that a person has made a basic decision of orientation to God revealed in Christ.

The movement may be a feeling, thought, insight, or any one of a number of inner actions or reactions. It may be slight, barely noticeable, moderate, or overwhelming. Intensity is not important, but the direction is.

If the movement is *toward God, you experience what Ignatius of Loyola, founder of the Society of Jesus (the Jesuits), called consolation. You might feel*

Centered
In synch with God
Grounded
Alive and awake
Awed or grateful
Free

FAITH, HOPE, AND LOVE ARE GIFTS.

If the movement is *away from God, you experience what Ignatius called desolation. You might feel:*

Out of sorts
A sense of darkness or agitation
Everywhere or nowhere
Dull, as if going through the motions
Addicted
Separated from God, others, and your true self

YOU FEEL THE ABSENCE OF FAITH, HOPE, AND LOVE.

- *Both orientations can be used by God.*
- *Usually one comes after the other.*
- *In movements toward God, linger and appreciate.*
- *In movements away from God, turn to God and be honest.*

Noticing in the Congregation

Let us look at two movements of the Spirit: toward God and away from God. Can you describe the mood or feeling of the group?

If the movement is toward God:

- You might feel it as being centered in God, whether or not there is much activity
- Things seem to go well; people don't insist on their way
- There is a lightness, a sense of freedom
- There is a deep awareness of grace and gratitude, a sense of awe
- "Not us, but God working through us"
- Faith, hope, and love are gifts
- You can listen first, then plan and work

If it is away from God:

- You may be out of sorts, grumpy, anxious
- People bicker or don't seem to care
- There is heaviness, a sense of ought
- There is compulsive busyness
- You go through the motions, unaware of God
- "It's up to us, sink or swim"•
- You are emotionally or actually separated from God

Both movements can be used by God. Persevere in downswings, use the energy in upswings to praise God and work. If you are stuck in being up, you might wonder about denial of darkness. If all you know is down, you might wonder what you need to let go of. In movements toward God, rejoice, give thanks, do long-range planning, and start new ministries if God is calling you in that direction. Be aware of God's presence. In movements away from God, God is working to change things. Ask for an outsider to reflect on what is happening. Ask God for help. There may be energy in the pain to lead to something new, a new view of God's call.

How Do I Know It's God
We Hear, See, and Sense?

1. This word, call, direction, voice sounds like God. There is an objective nature about God that surpasses my subjective feeling and thinking. We can find a consistency in the character of God as revealed in Scripture, especially in Jesus Christ.

Question: Does this sound like God?

2. The subjective reaction is a gift from the Holy Spirit. It is consistent with other experiences I have had that are sheer gift. The experience may not be ecstasy, joy, peace, or love, but those gifts point to the one who gives them.

Question: Is this word, call, direction consistent with God's history with us?

3. The fruits are spiritual: love, joy, peace, patience, kindness, goodness, faithfulness, gentleness, and self-control. They come together as a package.

- We are centered with God and ourselves and in community with others.
- Love is not a compulsive busyness, but an interdependent relationship, mutual. It is not just feelings or an attitude, but action, being. We are connected to our nearest and dearest, to others in community that we may dislike, and to the poor and downtrodden.
- Peace or serenity may be the major sign. This is not a false peace that comes from having an answer, but the inner certainty that lasts through ups and downs. It is a deep trust in God that all shall be well despite what happens to me.
- There may be tears of joy, clarity, a sense of things coming together.

Question: What are the fruits?

(over)

4. Our will and the Spirit of God are working together. We are not willful, trying to make things happen that we cannot control. We are not willfully passive, but are doing the things we need to do. We are willing, both actively, in doing gracefully what it ours to do, and passively, in surrendering what is God's or another's to do.

Question: Are we willing? Is Jesus Lord?

5. We check things out with mature Christians and listen to their guidance.

Question: What does the larger community say?

How can you write a summary of these questions briefly so that you can remember?

Peer Group Format for

Case Study

Silence
The peer group holds the presenter and the presenter's structure in silent prayer with intention for this case to serve the work being done by the presenter in his/her structure.

Presentation & Social Analysis
Presenter gives a brief background and description of the current situation of event. The present-er states a reason for using the event and asks for help desired (10 minutes). The group asks questions for clarification and information only (5 minutes).

Silence
Group members attend silently to what has been presented and their own interior response. "What did you notice?" Read through the case study or make notes if desired.

Group Shares: 20 minues
Each person shares what he or she noticed. Then the group continues in conversation, staying with, savoring, and deepening into the event. They may draw on tools or questions of the analysis stage. The presenter is silent.

Response
The presenter responds to the group's conversation.

Theological Reflection: 15 minutes
Five-minute silence, praying, "God, help us to see you in this event." Afterward the group reflects together on the mystery of how God is emerging in this event. The presenter may speak first.

Contemplative Action
What might the presenter do now to join God's action? The presenter may summarize or close.

(over)

**Individual
Reflection:**
10 minutes

Each person reflects in writing on: "How does this case study inform the work I'm doing with my own structure?" The presenter considers the following: "What have I learned?" "What might I do next time?" "What skills do I need to cultivate or what personal issues do I need to address?" "Is an action clear to me?"

Group Work:
30 minutes

Return to the group to share individual reflections and continue practicing with skills.

Triads

Paul Holmer, theologian, taught that there are two kinds of knowledge: knowledge about and knowledge of. Knowledge *about* is information, ideas, theology, books read. Knowledge *of* is knowledge that touches our hearts and transforms us. Only the Spirit of God can help us with knowledge of. We are to know God and ourselves in this second kind of I/thou knowledge. Theologian Martin Buber described these two ways of knowing as "I/it" and "I/thou." We need both, but "I/thou" is the language of prayer, the relationship of loving God and neighbor.

Triads are one way of learning this second kind of knowledge, which might be called contemplative knowledge. To do this listening or paying attention is a skill and a gift. Pray for the gift. This sort of dialogue is not discussing or reporting, but one person facilitating another's noticing at a deeper level where God's presence and call are found. The focus is on God, not on fixing problems or correcting theology.

1. The *speaker* shares where he or she has noticed God. What is noticed may be exterior or interior, an idea, feeling, sensing, or intuition. The speaker also reports on prayer or prayerfulness, where he or she notices God. The speaker may notice how God responds to prayer. In short, the speaker reports on his or her dialogue with the living God, or God's absence.

2. The *listener* has three kinds of responses:

- *Ordinary encouraging noises*: mmm, ooh, aah. This is paying attention lovingly and prayerfully. You know you are on holy ground.
- *Evocative questions*: not for information, but to encourage the speaker to notice more. "When your heart was moved, what was that like?" "What is happening now as you recall it?" "Are you aware of God now?" There is no right answer. Several stock questions are: "Did you ask God?" "What was God's response?" "Where is the call of God in that?"

(over)

- *Contemplative remarks*: "You noticed God's presence or absence in the story." "When you talked about that, your face really lighted up. It seemed to me that there was great joy in you." "It's really frustrating when God seems to be absent."

3. The *observer*. You aren't part of the conversation at all. The speaker and listener shouldn't look at you.

- *Keep time*: Announce when time is running out ("you've got a minute to go").
- *Observe the speaker*: What is being said beyond the words? What questions might you ask? Where do you notice God? Observe the listener. How well does he or she track and reflect? How spirit-led is the listening?
- *Observe the process*: Where is the Holy Spirit at work in each, in the dialogue, in you as you listen?
- *At the end*, ask both speaker and listener to report on their experience, and then share your observations.

Dialogue

The word *dialogue* is widely used, mostly to mean conversation. I use it here to mean a special discipline of group discernment.

Many of us have been taught active listening, mirroring, or a similar technique for listening as partners or helpers. Basically the exercise consists of repeating a phrase the other person has said. (For example: "You don't want to go out now.") When this technique is mastered, the listener may paraphrase what the other said ("Not now"). Then the listener may feed back what he understands the underlying feelings to be ("You're really tired"). For a spiritual director, the feedback may concern what the director perceives God to be doing ("God seems to be calling you to rest"). In any case, the person speaking can correct what is said in response until the listener gets it right. The listener makes no suggestions about fixing the problem of the speaker and does not share the listener's own experience.

This exchange is obviously very different from the sort of conversation that goes on in an ordinary meeting. Peter M. Senge, who teaches at Harvard University, has described the practice of dialogue as one of the major methods for helping a team to become a learning team. He lays out his ideas in *The Fifth Discipline*,[1] and more elaborately in *The Fifth Discipline Fieldbook*.[2] There he quotes the physicist David Bohm, who says that atoms behave differently when they are slowed down. Instead of bouncing off each other, they start to flow in the same direction. Bohm says that this phenomenon may happen to groups that practice dialogue. In this practice the debating attitude wanes, and a collective mindfulness or awareness may develop. He describes an elaborate plan that may be useful for large or conflicted groups. I present a rather simple format that may begin with ordinary meetings.

The leader may introduce this exercise by saying that the group is going to learn a new way to discern, or to listen to each other and God. First, there will be silent prayer, then the question for dialogue will be stated, and then people may speak. The prayer will differ from congregation to congregation. Some like 20 minutes of silence, others a simple contemplation of

(over)

scripture with half a minute of silence; others like to sing a hymn or a chant. (Individuals may choose to remain silence.). Then the leader will ask that the person who speaks second and every speaker thereafter to paraphrase what the previous speaker has said, to that person's satisfaction, before speaking his or her own truth. Reminders may be needed for speakers who forget. After a while, when the leader perceives that people are listening, he or she may say that repeating is not necessary. If the group heats up so that people are interrupting, the leader calls for a song or a period of silence. Usually new ways of thinking about the problem or issue may emerge out of silence and listening. Then the group may shift into a faster planning mode, or reach consensus or vote.

My experience is that even very controversial subjects can be the topic of such dialogue without polarization and defensiveness. As an example, the decision that the church made in Acts 15 had some of the elements of this style of decision making:

1. The issue for decision was clearly understood. ("We believe that we shall be saved through the grace of the Lord Jesus, just as they will" [v. 11].)
2. People spoke out of their experience. ("There had been much debate [v. 7]. . . . Barnabas and Paul . . . related what signs and wonders God did" [v. 12].)
3. Others voiced what they understood God's desire to be. (Peter summarized the revelation to them that the Gentiles should be included [v. 7].)
4. There was silence. ("And all the assembly kept silence" [v. 12].)
5. The leader summed up the process. ("With this the words of the prophets agree" [v. 15].)
6. The council understood that God had been part of the process. ("It seemed good to the Holy Spirit and to us" [v. 28].)

During an ordinary meeting, the same awareness of the Spirit can be fostered in many ways. Structuring the meeting as a worship service shifts awareness. Having a person praying for the group as it meets is helpful. Asking a person to attend to the movement of the Spirit in the group, variously called a group discerner or spiritual director, helps the group attend. Checking in and sharing where the Spirit is in people's personal and professional lives is of benefit, because then the group may notice that the Spirit is moving in similar patterns corporately.

For instance, at a recent faculty meeting at Christos Center for Spiritual Formation for a program for congregational leaders, we all said, as we checked in, something about being in transition. In our individual ministries the same theme surfaced. As we talked about what issue was at the forefront for the student group, it was evident that we were seeing the same issue emerge. Then the question became, "What is God saying to us? How do we reflect this to the entire group of students and faculty alike?" Our awareness was not that of solving a problem like "What should we teach next?" Our awareness was of how God was moving in our midst.

Resources

Christos Program for Congregational Leaders
Christos, a center for spiritual formation in Lino Lakes, Minn., north of Minneapolis and St. Paul, grew out of a retreat ministry that began in 1978. In 1983 a program in spiritual direction began. Two spiritual direction and personal formation programs now run simultaneously.

Christos is the only program in the country training pastors to do spiritual formation in the parish for the whole parish. Other programs are organized around small groups and spiritual direction.

For information, call (651) 653-8207, write to Christos, 1212 Holly Lane, Lino Lakes, MN 55038, or send an e-mail message to christoscenter@wordnet.att.net or log on to www.christoscenter.org.

ChurchSmart Resources
ChurchSmart Resources is located in Carol Stream, Ill. The group's basic book is *Natural Church Development: A Guide to Eight Essential Qualities of Healthy Churches*, by Christian Schwarz.

For information write to ChurchSmart at 3830 Ohio Ave., St. Charles, IL 60174, call (800) 253-4276, send a fax to (630) 443-7929, or send an e-mail message to ChurchSmart@compuserve.com.

The Alban Institute
The Alban Institute publishes and sells books aimed at a readership of clergy and other congregational leaders, and provides consultation and training. For information, write to Alban at 7315 Wisconsin Ave., Suite 1250W, Bethesda, MD 20814-1318, call (800) 486-1318, send a fax to 301-718-1966, or send an e-mail message to PWalker@alban.org.

Spiritual Directors International
Spiritual Directors International can help you find a spiritual director in your area. The group can be reached at (415) 566-1560.

Friends General Conference Bookstore
This bookstore is the place to find Patricia Loring's books on Quaker spirituality (*Listening Spirituality*, vols. 1 and 2). Phone (800) 966-4556.

Spiritual Life Inventory
More information on the Spiritual Life Inventory chart can be found in chapter 2. The inventory is published by Personal Power Products. Janet Hagberg's materials (including her books listed in the bibliography) are available here. Write to the firm at 1735 Evergreen Lane North, Plymouth, MN 55441-4102, call (612) 551-1708, or log onto the Web site at www.personalpowerproducts.com.

Introduction

1. Peter Drucker, *Post Capitalist Society* (New York: Harper & Row, 1994), 60.

2. Donald Miller, *Reinventing American Protestantism* (Berkeley: University of California Press, 1997). Miller studies three newly organized, successful denominations. These churches offer much to help the spiritual life of adherents. They practice a very "flat" management style for clergy, in contrast to the mainline hierarchy of experts in teaching and power differential in governing.

3. Miller, *Reinventing*, 187.

4. The Myers-Briggs Type Indicator is the most widely used psychological "test" that reflects a person's personality type. Many books have been written applying this system to spirituality.

5. Eugene Peterson, *The Message* (Colorado Springs: NavPress, 1993). This paraphrase of the Bible does not include verse marking; therefore, verse numbers cited are approximate.

6. Peterson, *The Message*.

7. Wendy Miller, *Invitation to Presence* (Nashville: Upper Room Books, 1995).

8. Carolyn Gratton, *Guidelines for Spiritual Direction* (Denville, N.J.: Dimension, 1980), 42.

9. Gratton, *Guidelines*.

Chapter 1

1. Robert Wuthnow, *After Heaven: Spirituality in America Since the 1950s* (Berkeley: University of California Press, 1998). A sociologist looks at changes in spirituality.

2. Parker Palmer, *The Courage to Teach: Exploring the Inner Landscape of a Teacher's Life* (San Francisco: Jossey-Bass, 1998). Permission granted to reprint charts on pp. 100 and 102 of Palmer's book..

3. Lyle Schaller, *The Interventionist* (Nashville: Abingdon, 1997), 96. Schaller has inspired some of my ideas in the first column, while Elizabeth Lesser in *Spirituality in America* has provided ideas in the third column.

4. Friedrich von Hügel, *The Mystical Element of Religion*. (Greenwood, S.C.: Attic Press, 1961). This classic study was written a hundred years ago by a liberal Roman Catholic who practiced spiritual direction according to his findings that individuals and congregations needed balance.

5. Most of this material came from a tape of Phyllis Tickle's lecture at the 30th National Conference of Trinity Institute, 1999. Product of Triunity Productions, Parish of Trinity Church, New York. Tickle is an expert on religion in the press.

6. Doug Bannister, *The Word and Power Church* (Grand Rapids: Zondervan, 1999). Bannister puts the evangelical and charismatic experiences together and shows a fine appreciation for reaching out to younger generations.

7. Peterson, *The Message*, 514.

8. David Steindl-Rast. *Gratefulness: The Heart of Prayer* (New York: Paulist, 1984), 89.

9. Frederick Buechner, *Listening to Your Life* (San Francisco: Harper, 1992). An edited collection of daily meditations. The first week's selections are about listening to your life and listening to God.

10. Patricia Loring, *Listening Spirituality*, vol. 2 (Washington Grove, Md.: Openings Press, 1999), 3.

Chapter 2

1. My ideas have come from many sources. I have been frustrated by schemes of spirituality that describe such prayer stages as the traditional ones of vocal prayer, meditation, and contemplation. I have been put off by contemplatives who assume that one kind of contemplation is the highest form. I see Jesus and the rest of the New Testament as more interested in our maturing in love. Therefore, Sam Keen's book *The Stages of Mature Love* gives me the titles for stages. *The Evolving Self*, by Robert Kegan, has moved past thinking about stages of faith, Kegan has learned from psychologist Carol Gilligan's work with women's development and Jean Piaget's work on children's personality development. Kegan sees growth

as a cycle, moving from being alone to being in community until at stage 5 we are able to do both. Women seem to get stuck at stages that are communal, while men get stuck at individual development stages. For the church, Neil Hamilton's book *Maturing in the Christian Life* takes the story of the disciples and shows the historical development of their relationship with Jesus. Minneapolis writer Janet Hagberg's *Real Power* takes stages of leadership function, which I folded into the model.

One can find fault with any map, but if it is recognized as a map rather than as a reality, it can be helpful. When I listen to an individual, I make a quick assessment, and then listen to what God is doing. In the same way I assess the person's theological point of view and religious language. In practice, giving lay groups these charts has always proved helpful. Some clergy, particularly if they put no stock in hierarchies, will have trouble with them and need extra help interpreting them.

2. For using this exercise with a group, I tell the story of the disciples with chart 1 at hand. Stress that this is more like a story than a test. Ask people which part of the story they might identify with as a congregation. Give them individual time to work on this question, followed by sharing with a small group of three or four. Then ask at what stage the church stands, taking volunteers rather than going around the circle. There is usually a range, but as people give their reasons the group begins to agree. Then ask, "What might God be calling this church to next? Where is the natural stage of growth that follows? Might this chart confirm what we already know or feel at some level?" My experience is that usually the group quickly puts its experience and the diagram together and has a sense of God's call in general.

Chapter 3

1. Corinne Ware, *Discover Your Spiritual Type* (Bethesda: Alban Institute, 1995).

2. John Macquarrie, *Paths in Spirituality* (New York: Harper & Row, 1972), 38.

3. Macquarrie, *Paths*, 30.

4. Simon Tugwell, *Ways of Imperfection* (Springfield, Ill.: Templegate, 1985), 200. This collection of essays about lesser-known spiritual leaders down through the ages supplies a healthy antidote to perfectionism.

5. Jean-Pierre de Caussade, *Abandonment to Divine Providence*, John Beevers, trans. (New York: Doubleday, 1975), 39.

6. De Caussade, *Abandonment*, 74.

7. Kathleen Norris, *Amazing Grace* (New York: Riverhead, 1998), 284.

8. David Steindl-Rast, *Gratefulness*. A Benedictine brother takes orthodox theology and translates it for the mindset of the younger generations.

Chapter 4

1. Paul Tillich, *The New Being* (New York: Scribner's, 1955), 138.

2. De Caussade, *Abandonment*, 74.

3. De Caussade, *Abandonment*, 81

4. Samuel Miller, *The Life of the Soul* (Waco: Word, 1951), 21.

5. Alice Mann, *Shepherding the Spiritual Life of Congregations* (Alban Institute seminar booklet, Sept. 1996), 14. Originally in Martin Thornton, *Pastoral Theology: A Reorientation.*

6. Friedrich von Hügel, in Jerome M. Neufelder and Mary C. Coehlo, eds., *Writings on Spiritual Direction by Great Christian Masters* (New York: Seabury, 1982), 8.

7. Christian Schwarz, *Natural Church Development* (Emmelsbull, Germany: C&P Publishing, 1996).

8. Schwarz sells a survey, which he says is more accurate than one's intuition alone. His questions are tested to provide statistically relevant answers, like those of a psychological test. The test is especially helpful because it shows strong points and weak points, and gives some clues about what should be done first.

9. Peter Vaill, *Learning as a Way of Being* (San Francisco: Jossey-Bass, 1996). In the introduction Vaill talks about his concept of "permanent white water"—a continuing state of turbulence and change, comparable to the churning of breakers, rapids, or falls.

10. This is my adaptation of a chart in John Kotter, *Leading Change* (Boston: Harvard Business School, 1996). Kotter has two styles; I added a third based on my experience.

Chapter 5

1. John Calvin, *The Piety of John Calvin*, Ford Battles, ed. and trans. (Grand Rapids: Baker Book House, 1978), 56.

2. Ernest Larkin, *Silent Presence: Discernment as Process and Problem* (Denville, N.J.: Dimension, 1981).

3. Kathleen Norris, *Dakota: A Spiritual Geography* (Boston: Houghton, 1993), 94.

4. Steven R. Covey, *The Seven Habits of Highly Effective People: Restoring the Character Ethic* (New York: Simon & Schuster, 1989).

5. Norris, *Dakota*.

6. Tadd Dunn, *Spiritual Exercises for Today* (San Francisco: Harper & Row, 1991), 206-207.

7. Dunn, *Spiritual Execises*, 162.

8. Alcoholics Anonymous World Services, Inc., *Alcoholics Anonymous*, 3rd ed. (New York: Alcoholics Anonymous World Services, 1976), 86.

9. Alcoholics Anonymous, *Alcoholics Anonymous*, 3rd ed., 84.

10. Martin Luther, *Luther's Prayers*, Herbert Brokering, ed. (Minneapolis: Augsburg, 1967), 47.

11. This is my version of Jonathan Edwards's work as I found it in Gerald R. McDermott, *Seeing God: Twelve Reliable Signs of True Spirituality* (Downers Grove, Ill.: InterVarsity Press, 1995).

Chapter 6

1. Albert Schweitzer, as quoted in *A Treasury of Quotations* (New York: Seabury Press, 1975), 131.

2. Peter Vaill, *Learning as a Way of Being* (San Francisco: Jossey-Bass, 1996).

3. We have carried out our work at Christos, a Protestant center that trains spiritual directors. There is a description of the content in appendix E.

4. See, for example, appendix D, handout 8. Also Anita Farber-Robertson, *Learning While Leading* (Bethesda: Alban, 2000).

5. Friedman, Edwin H. *Generation to Generation: Family Process in Church and Synogogue* (New York: Guilford Press, 1985).

6. Heifetz, *Leadership without Easy Answers* (Cambridge, Mass.: Harvard University Press, 1994).

7. Eugene Peterson, *Working the Angles* (Grand Rapids: Eerdmans, 1987).

8. Peterson, *Working the Angles*.

9. My program "Stop, Look, and Listen," described in appendix B, offers one way to learn to pay attention.

Appendix D
   1. Peter M. Senge, *The Fifth Discipline* (New York: Doubleday, 1990)
   2. Peter M. Senge et al., *The Fifth Discipline Fieldbook* (New York: Doubleday, 1994).

Alcoholics Anonymous. *Alcoholics Anonymous,* 3rd ed. New York: Alcoholics Anonymous World Services, 1976. To 50 million people the 12 Steps of AA are codified spirituality. The book's fifth chapter, "How it Works," is often read in meetings and treated as scripture. Its description of how to "work" the steps is simple yet profound. The book includes a guide for prayer, meditation, and regular inventory.

Allen, Diogenes. *Christian Belief in a Postmodern World.* Louisville: Westminster John Knox, 1989. Allen suggests that Christians not retreat, but talk with and listen to postmodern people and recognize God in them and in other religions, without relativism.

Armour, Michael, and Don Browning. *Systems Sensitive Leadership: Empowering Diversity without Polarizing the Church.* Joplin, Mo.: College Press, 1995. A faculty member at an evangelical seminary put me onto this book. The stages of development of systems are intellectual, yet their material fits rather well with my charts. They are helpful in showing how salvation and spirituality are understood at different stages.

Bannister, Doug. *The Word and Power Church.* Grand Rapids: Zondervan, 1999. This book suggests how charismatics and evangelicals can get along, and shows how new, growing churches understand the younger generations and the postmodern world.

Blackaby, Henry T., and Claude V. King. *Experiencing God: Knowing and Doing the Will of God.* Nashville: Broadman and Holman, 1998. This is a popular book, and several of my evangelical directees have used it in groups. Grounded in scripture, the book includes practical exercises for listening. A good evangelical beginner's book.

Buechner, Frederick. *Listening to Your Life*. San Francisco: Harper & Row, 1992. This is an elegant editing of Buechner's writing for daily devotional use. It is liberal and poetic. The first week's quotations are among the best I've read about listening for God in your life.

Calvin, John. *The Piety of John Calvin*. Ford Lewis Battles, ed. and trans. Grand Rapids: Baker Book House, 1978. Battles did the translation of the Institutes from the Latin; here he translated from the more elegant French and arranges the text as blank verse. Ought to be in every Calvinist home!

Farnham, Suzanne, Stephanie McLean, and R. Taylor McLean. *Grounded in God: Listening Hearts Discernment for Group Deliberations*. Harrisburg, Pa.: Morehouse, 1999. Simple; presents theory and practice. I suggest that a fairly sophisticated group would like this book a lot, perhaps Episcopal parishes.

Farnham, Suzanne, Joseph Gill, R. Taylor McLean, and Susan Ward. *Listening Hearts: Discerning Call in Community*. Harrisburg, Pa.: Morehouse, 1991. The authors have boiled lots of research down to simple writing, and this approach would be useful for candidates for ministry. The trouble with this elegant approach: How do you discern God's will day by day after one leaves seminary and enters ministry and has no special group?

Foster, Richard J. *Streams of Living Water*. San Francisco: Harper & Row, 1998. The laypeople and clergy with whom I have used this book have liked it a lot. Foster describes five patterns (evangelical, social justice, charismatic, contemplative, and holiness) of spiritual streams. He tells great stories and is sympathetic to a wide variety of spiritual practices.

Gratton, Carolyn. *Guidelines for Spiritual Direction*. Denville, N.J.: Dimension Books, 1980. Carolyn taught at Duquesne's Institute for Formative Spirituality in Pittsburgh, Pa., and her small book is packed with material on formation.

Hagberg, Janet. *Real Power: Stages of Personal Power in Organizations*. Salem, Wis.: Sheffield Publishing, 1994. This book encouraged me to put organizational stages and personal ones together, even though the author didn't see it my way. Hagberg tells great stories about how people function as leaders, together with hints for growing.

Hagberg, Janet, and Robert Guelich. *The Critical Journey: Stages in the Life of Faith*. Dallas: Word, 1989. The authors have produced a simple masterpiece. They tell stories about each stage of faith, and give hints on how to know when you're stuck. Some people would put the "dark night" (or wall, or crisis) in a different place. This is standard fare for training spiritual directors in Minneapolis.

Hamilton, Neill Q. *Maturing in the Christian Faith.* Philadelphia: Geneva Press, 1984. Hamilton takes the story of the disciples from their time of living with Jesus to their reception of the gifts of the Spirit. The author opened my eyes to the idea that this historical development is much like stage theory.

Heifetz, Ronald A. *Leadership Without Easy Answers.* Cambridge, Mass: Harvard University Press, 1999. A long, detailed, fascinating book.

Johnson, Luke Timothy. *Living Jesus.* San Francisco: Harper & Row, 1999.This a good book to give to liberals who have been on the quest for what Jesus really said, and who have read only Marcus Borg and other "Jesus Seminar" enthusiasts on the topic. Johnson asks whether Jesus is alive. If he is alive, we read the Bible in a totally different way: as the community's witness so that we can know him better. I've used this book as an introduction to the New Testament for laypeople.

Keen, Sam. *The Passionate Life: Stages of Loving.* San Francisco: Harper & Row, 1983. Keen has differentiated his theory of stages from that of James Fowler. Fowler talks about cerebral function; Keen talks about love. Keen here gives a great description of how love, rather than faith, matures.

Kegan, Robert. *The Evolving Self.* Cambridge, Mass.: Harvard University Press, 1982. This is the text used by many in Minneapolis to teach spiritual directors and psychologists (at, for example, the Cenacle Center and Adler Institute). Kegan takes earlier theorists, particularly Jean Piaget, adds to it the work on women by Carol Gilligan, a specialist in women's growth, and lists five stages, nuanced differently for men and women. Men easily stay at the independent stages (2 and 4), whereas women stay in relationship stages. Kegan is also interested in the transitions from one stage to the next.

Kise, Jane A., et al. *Lifekeys.* Minneapolis: Bethany Press, 1996. Many books help people get in touch with their spiritual gifts: this is a good one to use with new members to help them find their call in the church and the world.

Kotter, John. *Leading Change.* Boston: Harvard Business School, 1996. My business consultant friends highly recommend this book—it is the standard text in their field. Simply written, with diagrams.

Lamott, Anne. *Traveling Mercies: Some Thoughts on Faith.* New York: Pantheon Books, 1999. Hilarious spirituality.

Larkin, Ernest. *Silent Presence: Discernment as Process and Problem.* Denville, N.J.: Dimension, 1981. An older text by a master. Simple and profound.

Loring, Patricia. *Listening Spirituality*, 2 vols. Washington Grove, Pa.: Openings Press, 1999. The first volume is about individual spiritual practices, the second about corporate practices. Loring is a Quaker, a graduate of Shalem Institute.

McDermott, Gerald R. *Seeing God: Twelve Reliable Signs of True Spirituality.* Downers Grove, Ill.: InterVarsity Press, 1995. The author has taken Jonathan Edwards's writings and brought them up to date. Elizabeth Liebert, head of San Francisco Seminary's program in spirituality, says that she gives this volume and Ignatius' autobiography together to students so that they can see how two spiritual giants discovered the same patterns independently.

Miller, Donald. *Reinventing American Protestantism.* Berkeley: University of California Press, 1997. Miller has studied three "new paradigm" churches, and sees that a "flat" management style and a vital interest in spirituality go together.

Miller, Wendy. *Invitation to a Presence.* Nashville: Upper Room Books, 1995. I would think that this simply written book would be helpful for a group starting off. A guidebook for leaders is available.

Norris, Kathleen. *Dakota: A Spiritual Geography.* Boston: Houghton Mifflin, 1993. This is elegant writing by a secular woman finding her way back into the church, worshiping with Benedictines, preaching to Presbyterians, and finding God in the austere reaches of the Dakotas.

Olsen, Charles. *Transforming Church Boards into Communities of Spiritual Leaders.* Washington, D.C.: Alban Institute, 1995. I recommend this book highly to begin helping reorient boards and committees. It includes many suggestions about how to turn boards and committees into worshiping communities, and how to help leaders deepen their spiritual life.

Palmer, Parker. *The Courage to Teach: Exploring the Inner Landscape of a Teacher's Life.* San Francisco: Jossey-Bass, 1998. This book describes a new orientation to teaching, and it fits with Peter Vaill's book on mutual learning.

Peace, Richard. *Contemplative Reading.* Colorado Springs: NavPress, 1998. Peace, a professor at Fuller Theological Seminary, has a knack for writing usable guides to Bible study. This is one of four new books by NavPress that are simple introductions to a more contemplative spirituality. Readers are introduced to a classical way of studying a text, then a contemplative one. This book would be useful in most congregations.

Peterson, Eugene. *Working the Angles*. Grand Rapids: Eerdmans, 1988. Peterson shows the necessity for and the practices of prayer, spiritual reading, and spiritual direction. I use this with a companion book by Peterson, *Under the Unpredictable Plant,* for Doctor of Ministry classes. It recommends not only personal piety but also vocational spirituality for clergy.

Rendle, Gilbert R. *Leading Change in the Congregation: Spiritual and Organizational Tools for Leaders*. Bethesda: Alban Institute, 1997. Makes a helpful distinction between "management" and "leadership." Deals with spiritual, intellectual, and emotional elements.

Schaller, Lyle E. *The Interventionist*. Nashville, Abingdon, 1997. What caught my eye was the chart contrasting two styles of American churches—one growing and the other declining in membership. Schaller's material looks too simple at first, but when it is combined with the work of Parker Palmer, sociologists, and secular consultants, it appears that many people have seen the same pattern.

Schein, Edgar H. *The Corporate Culture Survival Guide*. San Francisco: Jossey-Bass. 1999. The author is known as the "father of corporate culture." His book helps the reader understand resistance to change.

Schwarz, Christian. *Natural Church Development*. Emmelsbull, Germany: C&P Publishing, 1996. A team of people researched 1,000 growing churches around the world and found that growth happens not because of some American technological gimmick, but because of eight natural areas that have been attended to. My only difficulty with the material is that the researchers don't talk about discernment. But used in tandem with my book, the material should be appropriate to most churches.

Smith, Gordon T. *Listening to God in Times of Change*. Downers Grove, Ill.: InterVarsity, 1997. What can this Canadian Baptist know? Plenty. He has studied with and now conducts seminars with a Jesuit scholar who is an expert on discernment. A good introduction for practically anyone.

Steindl-Rast, David. *Gratefulness: The Heart of Prayer.* New York: Paulist Press, 1984. In this densely written book, a Benedictine monk speaks the gospel in New Age language. A classic.

Thompson, Marjorie. *Soul Feast*. Louisville: Westminster John Knox, 1995. Thompson has done a wonderful job of writing an introduction to spiritual formation. It is clear and has depth and could be used in many ways in the congregation.

Tillich, Paul. *The New Being*. New York: Scribner's, 1955. Tillich's sermons kept me going through periods of darkness. The sermon on prayer is profound and simple.

Vaill, Peter B. *Learning as a Way of Being*. San Francisco: Jossey-Bass, 1966. Vaill teaches management and leadership in an MBA program, and sees the failure of most academic teaching to give leaders what they need: the ability to see that leadership is continual learning.

————. *Spirited Leading and Learning*. San Francisco: Jossey-Bass, 1998. The author tells secular leaders that spirituality is necessary for their own learning. Do clergy ever get this message?

Von Hügel, Friedrich. *The Mystical Element of Religion*. Greenwood, S.C.: Attic Press, 1961. Baron von Hügel was a liberal Roman Catholic layman who studied Catherine of Sienna, and saw three elements of religion. He taught balance in theory and in spiritual direction.

Ware, Corinne. *Discovering your Spiritual Type*. Bethesda: Alban Institute, 1995. Ware has taken the typology of the late Urban Holmes, and devised ways of teaching it. Leaders who want to teach their boards should use her test and carefully worked-out procedures.

Wuthnow, Robert. *After Heaven: Spirituality in America Since the 1950s*. Berkeley: University of California Press, 1998. Wuthnow, a sociologist, has done a lot of work on the sea change that the mainline churches, by and large, have not caught on to.